CURRICULUM, TECHNOLOGY AND TEXTUAL PRACTICE

EDITED BY
BILL GREEN

DEAKIN UNIVERSITY

This book has been produced as part of the study materials for ECS814 *Information Technology and Cultural Practice*, which is one of the units offered by the Faculty of Education in Deakin University's Open Campus Program. It has been prepared for the unit team whose members are:
Chris Bigum
Marie Brennan (consultant)
Lindsay Fitzclarence (consultant)
Bill Green (chair)
Penny Williams (developer)

The study materials include:
Chris Bigum, *Actors, Monsters and Cyborgs: Educational Practice in a Digital Economy**
Chris Bigum & Bill Green, *Managing Machines?: Educational Administration and Information Technology**
Bill Green, *Information Culture and Curriculum Theory**
Bill Green (ed.), *Curriculum, Technology and Textual Practice**
John Hinkson, *Postmodernity: State and Education**
Information Technology & Cultural Practice: Reader
Peter Medway, *Shifting Relations: Science, Technology and Technoscience**
Zoë Sofia, *Whose Second Self?: Gender and (Ir)rationality in Computer Culture**

*These books may be purchased from Deakin University Press, Deakin University, Geelong, Victoria, Australia 3217.
More titles may be added to this list from time to time.
Enrolled students also receive the following audiotapes:
Don Ihde, 'The Philosophy of Technology'
Elwyn Jenkins, 'A Teacher's Story'
Peter Medway, 'Technology and Education'

Published by Deakin University, Geelong, Victoria, Australia 3217
Distributed by Deakin University Press
First published 1993

Introduction and Concluding Note © Deakin University 1993

Edited, designed and typeset by Deakin University Publishing Unit
Printed by Deakin University

National Library of Australia
Cataloguing-in-publication data

Curriculum, technology and textual practice.
ISBN 0 7300 1620 X.

1. Curriculum planning. 2. Technology—Study and teaching (Primary). 3. Technology—Study and teaching (Secondary). I. Green, Bill, 1952-.
II. Deakin University. Faculty of Education. Open Campus Program.

375.66

Acknowledgments:
Photograph on p. 82: National Archives photo no. 306–NT–520A–6, reproduced by permission of the National Archives and Records Administration, Washington, DC; chapters 1–7 and the Postscript, © the authors, reproduced by permission.

Cover illustration:
The cover illustration draws upon the figure of the fractal, perhaps the most arresting icon of the emergent information culture. It brings together mathematics, aesthetics and information technology in such a way as to signify a distinctive realisation of postmodern practices and epistemologies. Fractals both embody and are generated from dynamic reflexivity and complex contextualisations, seen by many increasingly as the hallmark of the postmodern condition. Educationally, fractals represent new imaginings of learning and knowledge, and new perspectives on classrooms and pedagogy.

Contents

Introduction

Bill Green

Within the general area of the study of information technology and cultural practice, this monograph aims to bring together debates in the areas of curriculum, literacy and technology. More broadly, the concern here is with taking into educational account the relationship between language and technology, particularly as this relationship is changing or otherwise being affected by the advent of the new electronic technologies of text, image and sound—the communications and information (r)evolution, in short.

The relationship between language and learning is now well documented, as is the crucial role of language in education more generally. Language is similarly widely recognised as fundamentally implicated in social processes of identity, authority and structuring. The relationship between technology and learning, and the role and significance of technology in education, is much less established. Similarly, until relatively recently, the cultural and historical importance of technology in human affairs and social practice was given little formal attention, certainly in education. Indeed, if anything, it was often seen as subsumed by, and the faithful shadow of, science, consistent with the educational privileging of theoretical and academic knowledge over more material and practical forms. There are clear signs, however, becoming more and more emphatic and forceful during the 1980s and carrying on into the 1990s, that this situation is changing: for various reasons, technology is becoming increasingly more important on the educational-political agenda. This is evident at both the policy level and the level of professional discourse. Indeed, it is appropriate to refer to a new emphasis on *technologising the curriculum*, although as yet it must be argued that this development is conceived within a limited frame of reference—in Australia, that which has been summarised as economic rationalism, together with a new emphasis on the nexus between intellectual training and information technology.

To complete this thumbnail sketch, the relationship between language and technology is becoming increasingly a particular focus of attention, especially with regard to and in the context of the information and communications technologies. There can be little doubt that language is being transformed in significant ways, as are our understandings of it. The convention has been established that language is realised in two modalities, that of speech and that of writing; now, with the advent of what has been described as 'electronic languages', together with a heightened visual emphasis in contemporary life, this two-term understanding of language is being modified and certainly unsettled. It is not enough to say, either, that what we are witnessing is a return to the oral tradition, or at least a renewed emphasis on spoken language, within the terms of such arguments as that of Ong (1982), for instance, in referring to 'secondary orality'. Rather, quite new realisations of language must be considered, something which has important implications for education and society, given the crucial structuring role that language plays in social and educational processes. It is worth observing, then, that to date little explicit attention has been given to the *changing* nexus between language and technology, specifically in the context of education.

Technology, language, education: these are the nodal points around which the essays gathered together in this monograph turn. They are intended as introductions to current debates in the area, and also as provocations to further investigation and enquiry. Although—with some exceptions—not written specifically with this monograph, and the course of study it is part of, in mind, I have directed their publication towards this end because it seems very clear to me, in retrospect, that there has been a consistent line of development between their original commission and this present context.

Firstly, bringing together academics working in the area of language and literacy education, technology studies and educational computing, and curriculum studies is an important move, since all too often there is a tendency to work in separate and distinct disciplinary fields, with little or no systematic communication or movement between them. I feel that it is particularly important, therefore, to encourage *interdisciplinary* work, perhaps especially when it comes to assessing the educational implications of media culture and the new information technologies, and more generally technocultural transformations of curriculum and literacy.

Secondly, my editorial privilege enables me to survey the scene that these essays mark out, as well as subsequent developments in the educational field, at Deakin University and elsewhere, and to see them accordingly as both gesturing towards and representative of what is arguably the most significant politico-intellectual development of all, namely what has been summarised as the 'modernism/postmodernism' debate. Several Deakin University publications in recent years, most notably Giroux (1990) and Hinkson (1991), specifically address this debate, and there is a growing awareness that the field being mapped out in a course such as this is what is perhaps appropriately described as *postmodern educational culture*, or the emergent scene of *postmodern education*. Lyotard's (1984) treatise on 'postmodern' knowledge conditions is widely recognised as a crucial reference point for such enquiries. However, in recent years there has been an explosion of articles, monographs, conferences and books exploring this debate, and arguing its pros and cons. The durability of the debate is still in question; its current significance, I submit, is not. Hence, there is a need to grasp something of what it involves, particularly in its educational implication and applications.

What is particularly noticeable about the accounts of postmodernism and postmodernity provided by educators such as Hinkson and Giroux, and others such as Lather (1991) and Wexler (1987), is the recognition of, on the one hand, *language* and, on the other, *technology* as key features. This recognition is echoed, reinforced and elaborated in the work of writers such as Haraway (1991) and Poster (1990), drawing respectively from the fields of feminism and social theory. Similarly, and relatedly, the heightened significance of cultural considerations, of culture itself, has been described as crucial in understanding 'the postmodern turn' or the 'postmodern condition'; as Featherstone (1989, p.202) indicates, there are a range of meanings to be associated with the pairing modernism–postmodernism but 'common to them all is the centrality of culture' (see also Jameson 1984). New relationships between, and new forms of, culture and economy are also significant in this respect, and here it is appropriate to point to debates around the notions of 'post-Fordism' or 'neo-Fordism' (Robins & Webster 1989) as more industrial-economic registers of the postmodern. Featherstone (1989, p.197) usefully makes the following distinctions, in seeking to 'work towards some preliminary sense of the meaning of postmodernism':

modernity/postmodernity
modernisation/postmodernisation
modernism/postmodernism.

Frow (1991) proposes a similar formulation:

> In order to clarify matters you might want to distinguish between three conceptual moments: *modernism* (a bundle of cultural practices, some of them adversarial); *modernization* (an economic process with social and cultural implications); and *modernity* (which overlaps with the modernizatiuon process, but which I understand as a philosophical category designating the temporality of the post-traditional world). The same distinction of ontological levels holds good, *mutatis mutandi*, for post-modernism, post-modernization, and post-modernity. (Frow 1991, p.139)

As he observes: 'The point is not to grant autonomy to these moments but to make possible their more complex and contradictory articulation' (Frow 1991, pp.139–40).

This is not the place to elaborate on these matters; it must suffice simply to indicate the terms and lines of debate, and some sources of information in this regard. The point is: all this means that education, curriculum and schooling—the last two terms referring to what are arguably modernist concepts and projects *par excellence*—need to be re-considered and indeed re-assessed in the light of such arguments, and new reckonings taken into account consistent with the notion of the postmodern. The essays gathered here are not necessarily explicitly addressed to this task, although several are very much shaped and motivated by such an awareness. Nonetheless, framed in this way, they are likely to serve as introductions to these kinds of debate and argument, gesturing as they do in various ways towards some of the rivalries and relationships to be observed currently between 'modernist' and 'postmodernist' projects and perspectives in educational studies.

Some scene-setting is needed, at this point; some sense of context and occasion for the monograph as a whole. The essays gathered together here were first presented at a one-day seminar held at the Institute of Educational Administration in Geelong, on 25 July 1989. I had somewhat naively and foolhardily proposed the idea of the seminar some months previously, prior to taking up my new appointment in what was then the School of Education at Deakin University. This appointment represented quite a significant shift for me, not just geographically but also professionally. From a long-time research involvement in English curriculum studies and related forms of teacher education, I was moving (in all due fear and trembling ...) into an educational computing and technology studies context, my brief being to develop new research and teaching programs in the area of curriculum theorising and literacy studies, with specific reference to the new information technologies. Something of my own story is indeed relevant here, since in entering into what was at the time a new area of research and teaching, I was in much the same position as many curriculum workers currently—teachers, administrators, teacher educators, researchers, and so on—confronted by the increasingly significant nexus between education and technology. My appointment, then, and the seminar which occasioned this present monograph, were at once symptomatic and an attempt to stake out a territory, to claim some ground for critically assessing and evaluating the emergent cultural and educational scene, and to intervene in the new agendas increasingly organising and driving educational policy and practice.

The original seminar was, as I now recall, something of a baptism of fire for me personally and professionally. I had only recently shifted across the continent (exactly twenty days previously, as it happened). I was excited, yes, but also apprehensive, to say the least, and unsettled too. The expression 'Go west, young man' kept ringing somewhat ironically in my mind in those early hectic times—something associated with the pioneering spirit and the romance of the frontier, in what is perhaps a peculiarly American mythos: the West as the legendary land of promise and possibility. And there I was, shivering in the strange chill of a Victorian winter, having gone east ... Despite this, I observed, in the opening address to the seminar: 'We stand, I believe, on the edge of a new beginning, a Brave New World ... (and yes, I intend the irony)'. That ambivalence, that double sense which cannot be simply resolved once and for all, one way or the other—the connections to be made between 'technological dream' and 'technological nightmare' (Davenport 1990, p.113)—remains, even now, as an organising principle for our present lines of enquiry regarding technology, culture and education, and for engaging and understanding the changed and changing social conditions which increasingly inform and drive our lives and our work, as educators and as citizens alike in this last decade of the twentieth century.

Curriculum, textual practice, technology: the original seminar was conceived above all else as a *generative* occasion, and hence as initiating and inaugurating a continuing project, certainly one which extended beyond our gathering-together then and our being-there. In short, the aim was to explore some new ideas and forge some new connections—to engage with the 'new' ... This remains the ambition and the aim of this monograph, as what I hope will be an opening move in a continuing research and pedagogic conversation.

As with this monograph, the original seminar was organised in three parts, each intended to focus on one of the key terms ('curriculum', technology', textual practice'). The aim was to explore this focus in the context of, and in specific relation to, the other two terms. Figure 1 provides a graphic outline of the relationships.

Figure 1
Relationships among curriculum, technology and textual practice

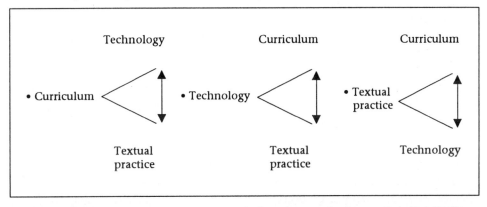

As it happened, connections tended to be made in an implicit rather than an explicit way at the seminar, something which is also evident in the essays gathered here. It remains the case, however, that it would be still a profitable exercise to work one's way systematically through each of these conceptual fields, that is focusing on 'curriculum', 'technology' and 'textual practice' respectively and in turn, in themselves and in their inter-relationship.

Some of the essays were written specifically for the original seminar and are essentially in the same form as originally prepared and presented. By and large, I have not attempted to update them (for instance, in their referencing), since they can usefully serve as markers and indeed as embodiments of the journey that readers must make in coming to terms with the issues in question here, especially those engaging such debates for the first time. Other essays were rewritten over an extended period of time subsequent to the seminar, some to the point of being new productions altogether. Reconciling the original seminar with this monograph has presented some difficulties, since the purpose and audience of each obviously differ considerably, in important respects. In the end, I decided against enforcing any neat or artificial reconciliation, since that might well have done violence to the pedagogic function of the present volume. Its somewhat 'archaeological' character should be borne in mind, however; different times and spaces co-exist here, as do different moments and trajectories in the uneven development of a series of arguments. In some cases, the writers have moved on considerably in their own thinking, and readers are encouraged to follow up their more recent work, as well as other related work.

For instance, the 'dialogue' between Ian Reid and Frances Christie presented here needs to be seen in the context of a larger series of debates in literacy pedagogy over the course of the 1980s, as indicated in their respective texts. The different positions here on literacy pedagogy—one informed by literary studies and poststructuralist theory, the other by educational linguistics—have subsequently been further refined and elaborated. Hence, it needs to be borne in mind, for example, that the educational-linguistic project that Christie's essay outlines, originally presented in July 1989 and revised for publication in 1990, has since been developed considerably further, in a number of important respects. For information on this and related matters, readers are advised to consult the Christie Report, available from the Centre for Studies of Language Education at Northern Territory University (Christie et al. 1991); with specific regard to the relationship between technology and textual practice, Section 4.9, 'New literacies for new technologies' (pp.211–25), is obviously apposite.[1] The value in this context of the essays by Reid and Christie is that, while they are not in themselves so directly addressed to actual technological transformations of literacy, they present strong and informed perspectives on literacy pedagogy which differ markedly from those which, to date, have been more commonly associated with the literacy-and-computing area. Much has been made, for instance, of the congruencies between computing and 'process' perspectives in writing pedagogy—new emphases, for instance, since the early 1980s and even the latter part of the 1970s on drafting and revision activities in composing, as well as on presentation and publication. Wordprocessing and desktop publishing are certainly important resources here. Linked to this development, there has been a predominantly cognitivist emphasis in both computing and literacy pedagogy, evident in research and pedagogy alike (e.g. Daiute 1985). While such lines of enquiry and investigation clearly warrant further attention and elaboration, they need also to be supplemented and complemented by other orientations, such as the rhetorical perspective offered here by Reid and Christie's educational-linguistic account of genre.[2]

I want to acknowledge both the substantive contributions *and* the patience of the contributors to this volume. With one exception, they were at the time of the original seminar all new colleagues of mine at Deakin University: Stephen Kemmis, Lindsay Fitzclarence, Chris Bigum and Frances Christie in what was then the School of Education, and Ian Reid from the

---

[1]   For a further account of the notion of 'text as technology', along similar lines of argument, see Martin (1990).

[2]   For a relatively early application of computing to 'genre' perspectives on literacy, see Pendreigh (1990).

then School of Humanities. Frances Christie has since moved on to become Professor of Education at Northern Territory University, and Ian Reid has moved across to Western Australia as Deputy Vice-Chancellor (Arts, Education and Social Science) at Curtin University of Technology. The exception was Peter Medway, then of the University of Leeds in the United Kingdom and now of Carleton University in Canada, who at the time was visiting Australia; his work on language, technology and English had been an important influence on my own thinking in these areas—something which continues to be the case, I am pleased to say—and hence I particularly welcomed his participation and his contribution. Indeed, I have learned much from all the contributors to this monograph, and I hope that its readers will similarly feel that, gathered together in this fashion, they represent an exemplary educational and scholarly resource.

References

Christie, F., Devlin, B., Freebody, P., Luke, A., Martin, J.R., Threadgold, T. & Walton, C. (1991), *Teaching English Literacy: The Preservice Preparation of Teachers to Teach English Literacy*, vols 1–3, Centre for Studies of Language in Education, Northern Territory University, Darwin.

Daiute, C. (1985), *Writing and Computers*, Addison-Wesley, Reading, Mass.

Davenport, E. (1990), 'Dreams and nightmares: Technology in 3-D', *Philosophy of the Social Sciences*, vol.20, no.1, pp.110–26.

Featherstone, M. (1989), 'In pursuit of the postmodern: An introduction', *Theory, Culture and Society*, vol.5, nos 2–3, pp.195–216 (special issue on postmodernism).

Frow, J, (1991), 'What was post-modernism?', in I. Adam & H. Tiffin (eds), *Past the Last Post: Theorizing Post-Colonialism and Post-Modernism*, Harvester Wheatsheaf, New York.

Giroux, H. (1990,) *Curriculum Discourse as Postmodernist Critical Practice*, ECS802 Curriculum Theory, Deakin University, Geelong, Vic.

Haraway, D. (1991), *Simians, Cyborgs, and Women: The Reinvention of Nature*, Routledge, New York.

Hinkson, J. (1991), *Postmodernity: State and Education*, ECS802 Curriculum Theory, Deakin University, Geelong, Vic.

Jameson F. (1984), 'Postmodernism, or the cultural logic of late capitalism', *New Left Review*, no.146, pp.53–92.

Lather, P. (1991), *Getting Smart: Feminist Research and Pedagogy with/in the Postmodern*, Routledge, New York.

Lyotard, J.-F. (1984), *The Postmodern Condition: A Report on Knowledge*, trans. G. Bennington & B. Massumi, University of Minnesota Press, Minneapolis.

Martin, J. (1990), 'Literacy in science: Learning to handle text as technology', in F. Christie (ed.), *Literacy in a Changing World: Educating for Language Proficiency*, Australian Council for Educational Research, Hawthorn, Vic.

Ong, W.J. (1982), *Orality and Literacy: The Technologizing of the Word*, Methuen, London.

Pendreigh, B. (1990), 'Computers and genre: A pedagogy of empowerment', in A. McDougall & C. Dowling (eds), *Computers in Education*, Elsevier Science Publishers, Amsterdam.

Poster, M. (1990), *The Mode of Information: Poststructuralism and Social Context*, Polity Press, Cambridge.

Robins, K. & Webster, F. (1989), *The Technical Fix: Education, Computers and Industry*, St Martin's Press, New York.

Wexler, P. (1987), *Social Analysis of Education: After the New Sociology*, Routledge & Kegan Paul, London.

Curriculum, technology, textual practice: Images and issues

Bill Green

Introduction

One of the most important developments in educational theory and practice in recent times concerns the question of technology, most notably but not at all exclusively new developments in information and communications technology. This development will inevitably require, as many have observed, decisive shifts in how we think about and conduct curriculum and schooling, at every level. It will also lead to new problems for research, policy and school practice. Our concern in this monograph is to focus on and explore the relationship among curriculum, technology and textual practice, within the context of these and related changes in education, culture and society at large.

Of particular interest is the educational significance of new theoretical emphases on information, language and the Symbolic Order, involving recent debate on what has been variously discussed as 'the postmodern condition' (Lyotard 1984), the 'cyborg' imagination (Haraway 1991) and 'the mode of information' (Poster 1990b). These theoretical and political initiatives are likely to have a considerable impact on educational discourse, and may well be particularly helpful in revisiting, and I hope rethinking, various current-traditional issues of curriculum concern, within which contemporary notions of language, meaning, textuality and framing have important implications. Within these initiatives, of particular concern is the crucial role and significance of the new information technologies, directly linked to which is more broadly the computerisation, metaphorical and otherwise, of curriculum and culture.

In particular, we are concerned here to bring together, in a productive way, what are all too often disparate areas of research and pedagogy: *curriculum* studies, *literacy* research, and—a subject that is becomingly increasingly important on the educational scene—*technology* studies. As far as technology studies is concerned, as already indicated, the emergence and proliferation of new information and communications technologies is of particular interest, and is a development which is likely to have quite decisive implications and consequences for the social practices of reading, writing and learning (Hirst & Woolley 1982)—that is, for curriculum and literacy, in the context of what might be called the transitional social space of postmodernity.

In what follows, I shall do two things. Firstly, I shall explore some of the images and issues involved in what has been very usefully called 'the technological imagination' (de Lauretis, Huyssen & Woodward 1980). This exploration will entail consideration of some technologically informed and textured notions of utopia and dystopia, as well as dreams and scenarios, science fiction and the technological unconscious: images of (im)possibility. I shall then extend such considerations into a brief exploration of the metaphorology of light and technology, pointing to some of their social effects and cultural consequences. In this first section of the chapter I will be operating in the mode of the poetic and the mythic, prior to shifting into a more expository and analytical account. My aim in operating in this way is, in part, *evocation*: an invitation to wonder and imagining. Secondly, I shall then move on to discuss aspects of language, technology and education, with reference specifically to the various 'technologies' associated with curriculum and literacy.

Images of the technological sublime

Jacques Derrida concludes one of his most generative essays ('Structure, sign and play in the discourse of the human sciences'), with reference to 'the as yet unnameable which is proclaiming itself and which can do so, as is necessary whenever a birth is in the offing, only under the species of the nonspecies, in the formless, mute, infant, and terrifying form of monstrosity' (Derrida 1978, p.293). Derrida's essay was originally published in English in 1967, but it may be that it is only now, as we enter into the final decade of the twentieth century, that we can begin to grasp the full implications and resonance of such a statement, as we live through the awe-full experience of epochal transformations and paradigm shifts in all their bewildering complexity, and as we career towards a 'new age'. The image of the 'monster', of some kind of 'monstrous birth', may well be most appropriate. What is it that awaits us, beyond tomorrow? What is it that is, even now, being born around us? Or is it the case, as some would have it, that we already inhabit the future?

It is hard to ignore the fact that the year 2000 is almost upon us. Once a distant goal, a glittering prize, an object of dreaming—like the Moon—it is now almost here, in all its super-charged significance. How shall we react to it, I wonder. We had a similar experience recently: 1984—now merely a memory, ever-receding. George Orwell's dystopian vision of the future is now safely in the past, it would seem; and, of course, as we now know, it was not 'true'. Somehow, despite all the dire forecasts, the gloom-and-doom prophecies—and conversely, despite all the utopian imaginings, of which names like Marshall McLuhan and Buckminister Fuller are symptomatic, to say nothing of Alvin Toffler—we managed to get through relatively unscathed, somewhat relieved, and yet perhaps also with a certain measure of disappointment. You know the sort of thing; like those terribly significant birthdays, those rites of passage; turning twenty-one, or thirty, or forty ... 'Is that all there is? We expect more of our representations, beautiful lies though we know them to be. We want them, somehow, to matter. We are torn between belief and desire, on the one hand, and on the other, a deep-seated, abiding scepticism: the double-sidedness of these dazzling times.

2000. 1984. Another date comes to mind, inevitably: 2001. Another cultural icon: Stanley Kubrick's film. With 1984 now safely behind us, and hence something of its mystique and significance lost, irrevocably, we might well wonder if that will be the fate of this extraordinary film too. What happens when the magical moment passes? Will the work continue to exert the same fascination for us, then, as it has now for the past two decades? Will it continue to speak to our dreams, our anxieties? These are, of course, questions that only history can answer; and time will tell, as it always does.

Two points are worth considering here, briefly. The first comes from juxtaposing Orwell's text and that of Kubrick, specifically in this present context. Both are instances of science fiction, richly imagined thought-experiments, projections into the future. Both are what Bill Nichols (1988) calls 'works of culture'. Yet one is a novel, the other a film. This is in itself a particularly significant matter, marking a major shift in our dominant forms of communication and culture—from the technologies associated with print and the book to those associated with film, television and other forms of video-textuality.

My second point is taken from *2001* itself: two exemplary moments. One is the famous scene where the transitional ape-like early humans come together in battle, and one discovers that the bone he has only recently realised as a tool serves also as a weapon, a club; flushed with victory, he hurls it up into the air—a supreme technological achievement, his weapon, the first symbolic moment in humankind's evolution towards the stars. Exultant, he hurls it high into the air and we, watching in the darkness, follow it up, up, and gaze in wonder as it changes into a spaceship, an enormous orbiting satellite, thus bridging millennia of human development. It is truly an extraordinary cinematic moment. A celebration of technology, however dark, it is also in itself a technological effect *par excellence*: a function of the cinematic apparatus. And yet, that this is the case, I suggest, scarcely registers ...

The other, of course, is Hal: the ultimate nightmare of the Machine taking over, caught up in its own (mis)readings of reality and assigning the humans in its company and its care to their extinction. And all so reasonably, too: 'Look Dave. I can see you're really upset about this. I honestly think you should sit down calmly, take a stress pill, and think things over'. The only thing that saves at least one of them here is transcendence, a metaphysical solution that does not really speak to the terror of Hal's psychosis and its evocation of what might well be called the technological unconscious.

I have referred previously to the notion of the 'West', playing on my own shift across the continent. But it is worth playing further with the notion here, because of its pertinence to the issues and debates that arise in considering the emergent field of language, technology and education. Certainly it calls to mind the images and genres of the Western, as a major and enduring feature of the American influence on cultural life, in Australia as elsewhere. We might well, accordingly, reconsider the role and significance of technology in the narratives and myths of the American West—the 'Wild West', as the tales would have it—and in doing so, make explicit connections between technology and nature; or rather, the technological domination and transformation of nature. I have in mind here not simply the revolver and the repeating rifle, and generally the technology of weaponry—significant though that is, as Paul Virilio (1989), among others, reminds us—but also, just as importantly, the development and expansion of new forms of communications technology, such as the telegraph service and the railroad (Carey 1989). In this light, we can also, and profitably, reconsider the colonialist dimensions of this whole matter, and note how the technological expansion of 'civilisation' has always involved, and indeed required, various forms of violence, symbolically but also quite literally—in the case of the American West, the buffalo and the tribes that once lived and died differently, in accordance with different rhythms and rules of being and becoming, and different dreams and forms of mapping and meaning. This observation might well, in turn, remind us that the domination of nature associated with modernisation and technological development has always gone hand in hand with the subjugation, the displacement and, in far too many instances, the wholesale destruction of other cultures and forms of civilisation and social organisation.

There is a particular pertinence in this for us, because an important theme for assessments of the role and significance of technology (and increasingly, the new forms of information and communications technology) in contemporary social life is the distinctive worldview associated with Western culture, seen by some as a dominant episteme. It is this worldview, manifest above all else in the *meta-rationality* of Western science and philosophy, which is increasingly being called into question as its consequences and costs become clearer, in such matters as 'the greenhouse effect' and the ever-present possibility of global armed conflict and nuclear warfare. Hence, arguments such as that of Simon During (1987) about the urgent need to forge political and theoretical links between the concepts of 'postmodernism' and post-colonialism are important, as are various arguments in feminism which increasingly interrogate contemporary techno-culture in terms of 'the informatics of domination' (Haraway 1991) and 'the death of nature' (Merchant 1980), within a new critical-holistic and eco-political framework of reference. At fundamental issue, as is becoming more and more apparent and urgent, is the very question of the survival of the planet and the sustainability of life itself, in all its various forms. In the context of a deliberate evocation of apocalypse, Iain Chambers makes the following observation:

It is perhaps unjust and imprecise to suggest that post-modernism merely entertains the idea of 'the end of the world'. More suggestively, and more accurately, it does suggest the end of *a* world: a world of Enlightened rationalism and its metaphysical and positivist variants; in a more immediate language, a world that is white, male, and Euro-centric, and which believes that its rationalizations are the highest form of reason. (Chambers 1986, p.100)

What this suggests is not just the significance of *post-colonialism* in and for reconsiderations of technology and contemporary culture, and the new information technologies in particular, but also the need to take into account matters of gender and rationality, and their associated politics.

The counter-posing of images of 'sunrise' and 'sunset', of 'East' and 'West', of 'light' and 'dark', is another matter worth pursuing. As Gregory Ulmer observes, following Derrida, light may be regarded as the philosophic metaphor *par excellence*. Hence, 'any change in our understanding of its nature should affect its analogical extensions in such concepts as form and theory' (Ulmer 1985, p.26), and indeed in thinking generally. This observation is echoed by John Hinkson's (1987) exploration of the cultural significance of the metaphor of 'sunrise industry'. Used almost universally, it is an image capturing the imagination in its evocation of a new era, a distinct new phase in civilisation and society. Hinkson cites Arthur C. Clarke's epic-visionary science fiction novel *Childhood's End*, in which humanity is portrayed as moving 'through a series of developmental transformations which emanate from a mystery source somewhere in the stars'. His paraphrase is worth quoting:

Our ape ancestors are manipulated into new levels of development always by processes bathed in blinding light. We are set on an epic adventure which carries the species stage by stage towards the stars. We falter in one phrase by an over-reliance on computer as mind. Eventually the hero steps beyond the frame of what we can grasp and transcends time, space and the body. Through the hero we achieve our ultimate state, amidst the light of the stars, as pure mind moving through space. (Hinkson 1987, p.144)

The links with *2001: A Space Odyssey* are obvious. Both participate in a myth of transcendence, of the intrication of emancipation and enlightenment. Kubrick's film opens with 'The Dawn of Man', with a landscape gradually bathed in light: a sunrise. This is echoed soon after by the literal image of 'sunrise on earth', seen from the vantage point of the spaceship, itself suggesting the dissociation of the subject from the body of the Earth. The film then proceeds to explore the inexorable movement towards the transcendence of humankind, a narrative movement thoroughly immersed in what Derrida (1978) describes as the metaphorology of light. Transcendence, enlightenment, emancipation: as Hinkson observes, these are deep-seated cultural assumptions in the general rhetoric of the information revolution. But it is not simply the advent of late-twentieth-century information culture that is at issue here. Rather, as Jameson (1984) argues, such developments need to be understood as the apotheosis of Western technologistic capitalism, with the so-called electronic revolution representing a heightened form of a new mutation in the multinational project of capital.

However, it is these very notions of emancipation and enlightenment, which Lyotard (1984) describes as 'meta-narratives', that arguably characterise and indeed drive the social project of modernity and, consequently, the discourse of modernism. They are necessarily linked concepts, bringing together the twin goals of knowledge and human freedom, and as such are deeply embedded in, for instance, the historical mission of modern(ist) schooling. We commonly refer to the liberatory possibilities and consequences of becoming knowledgeable, whether on the personal and individual level or on a grander, more collective scale. So, for instance, the campaign for universal literacy is linked to notions of progress and social development, because to become literate is, in this view, to gain access to knowledge and so to enable the shift from 'barbarism' to 'civilisation', from the 'dark' of ignorance and savagery to the 'light' of culture and knowledge. The ethnocentrism of such a line of argument is undeniable.

As Hinkson (1987, p.143) observes, 'light is a symbol of liberation and emancipation'. It enables us to see things truly or anew; it enables us to transcend, to go beyond and indeed leave behind, our base animal nature. More than this, even, it enables us to escape the shackles of nature altogether: 'one of the cultural meanings of technology has been its ability to liberate the species from the constraints of nature' (Hinkson 1987, p.143). Hence, there is a profound irony in the image of the 'sunrise', evoking as it does the sun as the supreme natural force. This is because what is at issue in the so-called sunrise industries is the paramount significance of *artificial light*, as associated principally with electricity. 'United in sunrise industry', Hinkson (1987, p.143) states, is 'emancipation through technology and emancipation through light', particularly and ever-increasingly that associated with electronics and electricity. James Carey and John Quirk provide a striking account of the importance of electricity in the development of modern society, describing it as linked decisively to modernisation ideologies and futurist myths of social and human progress, and hence as 'the motive force of desired social change, the key to the re-creation of humane community, the means for returning to a cherished naturalistic bliss' (Carey with Quirk 1989, p.115). For those holding to such a view (which they suggest remains the dominant one), 'their shared belief is that electricity will overcome historical forces and political obstacles that prevented previous utopias' (Carey with Quirk 1989, p.115). This they describe as a characteristic position in 'the rhetoric of the electrical sublime' (Carey with Quirk 1989, p.123).

Something of the contradiction of such views emerges here in the way the nature/culture dualism is deployed. While electricity, and technology more generally, has enabled the transformation and domination of nature and ultimately its transcendence, it has also often been presented as a return to nature, or at least to certain of its qualities. It has been presented in this way because, as the rhetoric has it, it provides humanity with the opportunity to realise its natural capacities and its potential: to become what it always-already is, innately, although this has been obscured by the long hard struggle out of darkness ... Carey's account of the telegraph is instructive and compelling in this regard, analysing it in terms of the relationship between technology and ideology. Describing it as 'one of the least studied technologies, certainly the least studied communications technology' (Carey 1989, p.201), he presents it as a decisive feature in the modernisation of the United States, bringing together monopoly capital, electricity-based industry, and the social and epistemological restructuring attendant on changed forms of communications technology. The central significance of electricity is made very clear. Observing that 'other technological marvels' were also developed in the course of the nineteenth century, Carey nonetheless sees the telegraph as distinctive in influencing a new worldview bringing together technology and electricity in a new rhetoric of 'the sublime', mixing elements of wonder, mystery and power:

> The key to the mystery was, of course, electricity—a force of great potency and yet invisible. It was this invisibility that made electricity and the telegraph powerful impetuses to idealist thought both in religious and philosophical terms. It presented the mystery of the mind–body dualism and located vital energy in the realm of the mind, in the nonmaterial world. (Carey 1989, p.206)

This theme of the 'invisibility' of technology—of 'invisible technology'—is crucial, as will be further outlined later in this discussion. For the moment, it is sufficient to note it here, and then to move on to indicate some of the effects of the telegraph, in particular its construction of a new relationship between geography and markets, its restructuring of time, and its 'colonisation' of the night.

This last point is especially apposite. Carey (1989, p.228) refers to 'the notion of night as a frontier, a new frontier of time that opens once space is filled'. Once again, the significance of light, and specifically electric light, is very clear. The availability of relatively inexpensive sources of electrical power enables more of the night to be used and indeed commercialised—itself transformed, that is, into both a market and a 'workplace'—as well as becoming more actively associated with the identity-work of the culture industries. In this way, what might be described as the natural rhythms of night and day are displaced and a new cultural rhythm established in their stead, bringing with it changed forms of social relationships. Once again, we are drawn to contemplate the waxing and waning of cultural forms, and also the ambiguity and ambivalence of light imagery in dominant discourses in technology and society.

A final point should be considered here. Ulmer, as has been previously noted, draws attention to Derrida's engagement with light as a concept-metaphor thoroughly imbricated in Western metaphysics. In particular, Derrida insists upon the need for a philosophical recognition of new developments in physics, specifically those associated with light as a field/particle/wave complex, and consequently argues for a post-Einsteinian reconceptualisation of conceptuality itself. Ulmer's own explorations of what this might mean for rethinking curriculum and literacy are extraordinarily suggestive, I believe, and well worth systematic investigation at the level of primary and secondary schooling. For the moment, it must suffice to note that light and more generally vision are clearly integral to literacy (understood for the moment simply as reading and writing), and similarly are necessary features of the screen-based forms of cultural practice and textuality associated with word processing and other forms of computer-based technology, which is something clearly central to the notion of new and emergent literacies.

Curriculum, literacy and technology

At this point I want to turn from these images and evocations to a more analytical account of curriculum, literacy and technology, as a more specific focus for this present exploration of the relationship between technology and cultural practice, more specifically in its educational implications. I shall begin, therefore, by outlining the territory. The title of the monograph is *Curriculum, Technology and Textual Practice*, and as titles go, it is a good indication of the ground in question as well as the work to be done. In other words, our particular concern in this monograph is with the network of relations among the categories 'curriculum', 'technology' and 'textual practice' (which for the moment can be described simply as 'textuality')—that is, the conceptual field that this network embraces. This conceptual field can be depicted as in Figure 1.

Figure 1

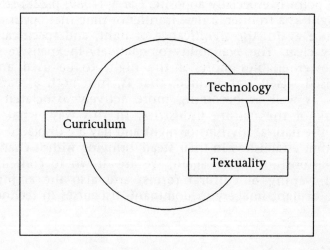

Within this conceptual field, my first-order concern is with the relationship between curriculum and literacy, and more generally with the relationship between curriculum theorising and literacy research, particularly with regard to new technological initiatives as they affect classrooms and schooling. The importance of these relationships, in my view, has been insufficiently recognised to date, and there is little sustained conceptual work specifically in this area. By and large, scholarship on, respectively, curriculum and literacy proceeds quite independently of each other. It is relatively rare to find a specialist curriculum scholar who really understands the nature, complexity and necessity of language and literacy practices (and more generally, the Symbolic Order) in and for curriculum, at every level, from the micro-exchanges of the classroom to the construction of national agendas. Similarly, specialist literacy research—currently burgeoning for reasons well worth contemplating, in a time of extensive educational restructuring and liberal-conservative restoration—tends not to problematise curriculum adequately, or to take its conceptual complexity into account in its own research. At best, 'curriculum' operates as a subsidiary concern in current-traditional forms of literacy research, and hence part of its context of presupposition. To a certain extent, of course, this is entirely understandable: a register of the institutional division of labour in the academy and elsewhere; a matter, that is, simply of focus and selection. Yet I want to suggest that strong classifications of this kind are counter-productive, and increasingly so. Rethinking the relationship between curriculum and literacy is crucial, then, in coming to terms with educational theory and politics more generally.[1]

Let us look at one example. There is an important relationship still to be adequately investigated between school writing and the 'reproduction' thesis in critical curriculum studies. Such an investigation would indicate very clearly, I suggest, that questions of language, knowledge, subjectivity and the body are quite fundamental curriculum-theoretical issues, as well as being matters of concern in and for literacy research, in ways that are scarcely recognised as yet. Perhaps more to the point, they are pertinent concerns for educational praxis, at every level. Schooling as a discursive-ideological practice operates not simply to initiate children into the culture of literacy, but also to incorporate them within the social field, to enter into and work on their bodies as social objects, and to establish and consolidate the complex, motivated field of their subject-positioning, the limits and possibilities of their identities and their agency: to shape and inform them, therefore, as body-subjects, and hence as individual consumers and citizens.

Further, in a manner yet to be fully appreciated, an important connection is to be observed between curriculum and literacy in that both, viewed in what is arguably the most appropriate manner, are organised by

---

1 This is precisely the project that informs a collection of papers that I have recently edited, with contributions from a range of literacy and curriculum scholars (Green 1992). A notable feature of the book is the absence of an account specifically focused on the implications of the new technologies for curriculum and literacy.

the problem of *meaning*. In the case of curriculum, what is at issue is the relationship between schooling as an over-determined ideological communication and the cultural production of the classroom, and therefore between student learning and the dynamics of cultural transmission and social reproduction. It needs to be recognised that this relationship is, above all else, a matter of 'meaning making', and hence of textual practice. Similarly, literacy needs to be emphasised as involving a heightened awareness—a meta-awareness, if you like—of the role and significance of rhetoric and textuality in education and the cultural field.

With regard to 'curriculum' and 'literacy', then, the linking factor is the concept and the problem of *meaning*; that is, both 'curriculum' and 'literacy' are concerned with matters and problems of 'meaning making'— in itself, something that might be regarded as a relative commonplace of contemporary mainstream research these days. However, it is still a matter far from being fully or properly understood, although it is true to say that it is becoming increasingly problematised, even as it becomes an important research focus in the wider field of scholarship and intellectual enquiry.

Given this assertion of a relationship of fundamental importance between 'curriculum' and 'literacy', on the basis of the common problem of 'meaning', we can ask: *what is changed with the introduction of the new technologies, particularly those involving computerisation, information and communication?* That is, how is 'meaning'—the nature of meaning, the conditions of meaning, the politics of meaning— changed, or at the very least influenced, by the advent of the new information technologies? Similarly (and indeed relatedly), what are the implications and consequences of new developments in linguistic and semiotic research, cultural studies and discourse theory for curriculum and literacy, given the challenge they represent to current-traditional notions of textuality, meaning and subjectivity? Further: what are the material conditions for this challenge? Among other things, the role of technology is particularly significant, as commentators such as Henry Giroux (1990) and others recognise in pointing to 'the increasingly powerful and complex role of the electronic mass media in constituting individual identities, cultural languages and social formations' (Giroux 1990, p.20), as well as 'the development of new technologies that have redefined the fields of telecommunications and information processing' (Giroux 1990, p.12).

A point that needs to be taken into account here is what various commentators are describing as a shift in emphasis and orientation from 'modernism' to 'postmodernism' as an explanatory principle for educational theory and practice (Lather 1991; Giroux 1990). Central to this argument is the thesis that what I am referring to as current-traditional forms of curriculum and literacy need to be recognised as central features of a general modernist project, organised by the meta-principles of emancipation and enlightenment. More specifically, we can understand campaigns for mass literacy as one of the most important elements in the social engineering initiatives of the modernist era (Donald

1983; Lankshear with Lawler 1987), as indeed is the institutional apparatus of popular schooling itself. Hence, we might well consider the value of introducing a distinctively 'postmodern(ist)' perspective on curriculum and literacy. More specifically, we can start thinking about the possibility of developing a theory of 'postmodern' literacy, one which is arguably more appropriate for the era we are living in and which our children will inherit.[2]

To this point I have been focusing on the relationship between curriculum and literacy, with less emphasis on the concept of technology itself. However, it is necessary now to turn to the relationship among the three more directly. Figure 2 is an attempt to depict how this relationship might be approached.

Figure 2

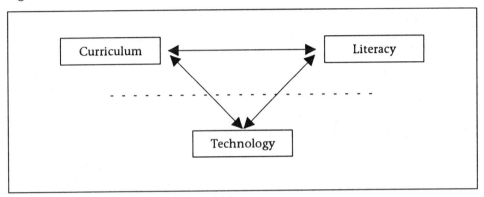

At this point, I must confess to a certain trepidation at the time of the original seminar, intermingled with the excitement of entering into a new field. The trepidation stemmed from the fact that, for me and I suspect for many others as well, the whole business of technology—particularly in its educational significance and application, and even more specifically with regard to information technology, especially computing—was, and possibly remains, a new and somewhat frightening venture. Hence, the title of the seminar ('Curriculum, Technology and Textual Practice') worked conceptually on the basis of what can be called, playfully, an 'excluded middle', a central absence. What was missing, essentially, was the very notion of 'technology' itself, as a matter needing to be placed much more squarely on the agenda.

On reflection, however, it became clear to me that, far from being a personal 'lack' for many educators at the present time, a proper sense of 'the technological' is, by and large, missing—absent? excluded?—in both curriculum studies and literacy research in their current formulations. Put

---

2   Whether one refers to a 'postmodern literacy' in this fashion or to a 'postmodernist account of literacy' is a matter worth considering; for a similar point concerning the notion of 'a postmodern sociology' (as opposed to 'a sociological account of postmodernism'), see Featherstone (1988).

more strongly, I propose that the whole question of technology has been either forgotten or else actively repressed in such work to date. What do I mean by this? On the face of it, such a claim may seem provocative and even scandalous, if not altogether and simply 'wrong'.

For instance, there has been much recent discussion and debate about the challenge of 'the new technology', particularly that associated with computing, and, perhaps needless to say, there has been a correspondingly heavy investment of time, energy and resources (monetary and otherwise) in new technological initiatives in schools and other educational settings. There is no doubt that this investment is both warranted and legitimate, to a degree at least, in that there has clearly been a proliferation of such developments in recent times and an ever-increasing complexity and sophistication, and a corresponding need for such investment. Put simply, there are undeniable and important socioeconomic imperatives behind such moves in educational policy and practice.[3]

I cannot help wondering, however, if there is a very real risk of falling into the trap of technological fetishism. Consider, for instance, our fascination with the computer, as the most visible icon of the new technology. A very real danger exists, I believe, that technology is seen merely in empiricist-objectivist terms—that in the most limited sense we focus all our energies on material-objective forms of technology. Computers are clearly instances of what might be called *techno-objectivity*; they are markedly and manifestly 'techno-objects', or 'machines'. Attention is therefore compelled to the technology as a 'thing' in itself—the 'nuts-and-bolts', so to speak—the very materiality of a work-station (in a manner analogous perhaps to the television set): that object which sits on our desks or otherwise occupies space in our offices, our laboratories and our classrooms. However, this is an extremely limited and reductionist way of thinking about computers in particular and more generally (information) technology. We need to consider them always in context, in terms of social relations and cultural consequences and meanings, and hence we need to understand the all-important relationship between *material technologies* and *cultural technologies*, as well as the conceptual distinction between them. The computer as a 'social object' cannot be dissociated from questions and considerations of the 'social meanings' and 'social forces' that are a necessary part of the proper contextualisation of computing as a sociocultural activity.

Consequently, the especially important point about the introduction of computer-based technology into our classrooms and our lives may be that it has served to render visible and palpable, and hence bring to a conscious level of awareness, what had previously been hidden or otherwise rendered invisible. (Consider, in this light, my earlier reference to the scene from Kubrick's film, where the spinning bone is transformed into a spaceship—a particularly good instance of the invisibility of technologies, as I suggested.) Knowledge—the production and

---

3   This is not to say that the social and political meaning of these initiatives and imperatives is either straightforward or beyond criticism and dispute; quite the contrary.

transmission of knowledge—has always involved technologies of various kinds. Furthermore, it can be argued that, outside the operation and application of what might be called *cultural* and perhaps more specifically *curriculum* technologies, school knowledge simply does not and cannot exist. That is to say, knowledge has necessarily a complex material and institutional mode of existence.

I want to explore this notion at this point, albeit briefly, with reference to an argument developed by Ian Hunter (1984), drawing on the later Wittgenstein.[4] Hunter observes that our knowledge of colour terms and discriminations—our colour knowledge generally—cannot be dissociated from the availability of specific institutions, practices and techniques, which he brings together in what can be called here the concept-metaphor of 'technology'. In this neo-Wittgensteinian perspective:

> ... we can form a picture of human beings as bearers of a dispersed array of practical capacities. These are built up through piecemeal mastery of a patchwork of social technologies ... They possess no general form or condition of possibility, save those found in actual forms of social organization. (Hunter 1984, p.420)

Hunter gives the example of what it means to speak of 'reddish yellow' rather than, for instance, 'bluish yellow', linking the activity of understanding in this regard to 'the technique of "choosing a colour from a set of examples" ' (Hunter 1984, p.418). Moreover, as he indicates, the available 'technologies' are both limited and culturally specific: he cites as examples 'the colour wheel, the graduated palette, the rainbow' (Hunter 1984, p.418). As he observes, 'capacities for identifying colours and understanding the meaning of colour terms are local accomplishments resulting from the practical deployment of technologies such as the colour wheel'; and further: 'differences in colour concepts' relate to 'differences in available technologies' which, significantly enough, he designates as 'language games' (Hunter 1984, p.419). Finally, our capacity to *imagine* new colour terms and combinations—and similarly, it might be argued, new forms of curriculum and literacy—is constrained by the existence and availability of 'different but definite social technologies. Our imagination is limited to those we have a practical familiarity with and those we can construct by analogy' (Hunter 1984, p.420).

My interest in this argument, which of course I can only summarise here, is fuelled by my feeling that it usefully illuminates how 'technology' might be conceptualised with regard to curriculum and literacy—or rather, somewhat more cautiously, how the category 'technology' might be deployed to good effect in this regard. Examine, for instance, the

---

4 Regarding the pertinence of this argument to the relationship between literacy and technology, I am indebted to discussions with Elwyn Jenkins on this and related matters, in the preparation of his Honours dissertation under my supervision (Jenkins 1988).

following definition of literacy, in itself overall an enlightened and generative account:

> ... the abilities to read and write are acquired through culturally specific, formal and informal systems of pedagogy. Hence, literacy can be considered a 'set of socially organized practices which make use of a symbol system and a technology for producing and disseminating it' [Scribner & Cole 1981, p.236]. Practices of literacy and the very material form of the technology (e.g. script, typography, teletext) undergo historical evolution, as do attendant sets of educational practices for the teaching of literate competence ... Different cultures and subcultures, in different historical epoches, have generated distinct modes for the dissemination of literate competence. But while a technology in theory at least may be neutral, modes of training in the use of a given technology invariably prescribe constraints upon and conventions governing that use. (Luke 1988, p.17)

What is notable here, and what I want to draw attention to, is the distinction posited between the concept of a 'symbol system' and that of a 'technology'. In one sense it is a useful point to make, because it is indeed the case that language is differently embodied in script, print and electronic image. However, what it can obscure is that the symbol system itself needs to be construed as what might be called a cultural arbitrary, a sociocultural artefact, and more generally as a cultural technology. To argue in such a way is to stress that the introduction of computers and other forms of information technology into our classrooms and workplaces needs always to be seen in historical terms, in a complex relationship with the social meanings and cultural consequences of such previous 'technologies' as the alphabet, written language and the printing press.[5]

A further point to consider in this context concerns the question of technology's 'neutrality'. Whether technology is neutral is certainly debatable, although it is true to say that by and large technology has traditionally been seen in instrumental terms, and as essentially neutral. The parallels with language are striking. C.A. Bowers (1988) has very usefully brought together debates and assumptions concerning language and technology in arguing for what, following the work of Don Ihde (1982, 1990), he considers the necessary *non-neutrality* of technology. He specifically links two questions: first, 'does technology mediate human experience in a way that reveals its non-neutral character?' and second, 'what are the implications of not accepting the conduit view of language that has its roots in the thinking of John Locke?' (Bowers 1988, p.27). The

---

5   Also, of course, the specific technologies associated with 'pen-and-paper'; see Monaghan and Saul (1987). With regard to language itself, Bowers (1988, pp.39–40) writes: 'Language is indeed a technology in that it involves the formalization of sounds and syntactical rules that enable people to communicate with each other. Printed language reveals even more directly the connection with technology; in its earliest form the crude markings that were the precursors of the alphabet were used as a technique for aiding in the memory of business transactions and military logistics.' See also Christie, in this volume.

'conduit view' of language that he refers to here is a longstanding feature not simply of popular opinion and commonsense but of philosophical orthodoxy, and involves seeing language as simply a means to an end, a container-like instrument for the transmission and storage of information, ideas and meanings. In such a view, thought is separate from language and is also prior to it; this has the effect of privileging the realm of thought, or consciousness, in a classic expression of 'representational thinking' and the rationalist tradition. The significance of language is effectively downgraded in such a view, as indeed simply a 'technology'.

Ihde argues, however, that technologies are inevitably 'transformative' and 'non-neutral' because, as he writes, 'not only does a technology contain in its use an invariantly transformative factor, but it does so in a specific way. Every technology has what I call a *telos*, or weighted center of gravity[,] that makes it partially selective as to what may be enhanced and what reduced' (Ihde 1982, p.64). He uses the notions of 'amplification' and 'reduction' as key terms in his account of technology, arguing that there is an inescapable *dialectic* of amplification and reduction involved in the application and use of any technology. That is, as Bowers (1988, p.32) puts it, 'the use of technology, in effect, amplifies certain aspects of human experience and reduces others'. Hence, 'the essential nature of the technology selects the aspects of experience that will be amplified and reduced. Thus technology is not simply a neutral tool, ready at hand, waiting to be directed by a human being'; rather, 'it acts on us (through selection and amplification), as we utilize it for our instrumental purposes' (Bowers 1988, p.32). Taking into account how specific technologies both amplify and reduce human possibilities and capacity—whether it be the clock, the bicycle or the microwave oven, or such instances of communications technology as the printing press, the telephone and the computer—is therefore a crucial move in assessing technology generally. It can be argued, furthermore, that the advent of the so-called new technologies of text, sound and image makes such assessments all the more urgent because the new relationship between language and technology that is associated with such developments has crucial and quite fundamental implications for reconfigurations of human identity and being, and social practice more generally (Hayles 1990).[6]

A central issue in the relationship between curriculum and literacy, as I have indicated elsewhere (Green 1993), is the 'speech/writing' debate: that is, the relationship between 'speech' and 'writing', and specifically whether they are to be seen in terms either of similarity or difference, and the implications the chosen view has for schooling and educational practice.[7] This whole issue needs to be recast more explicitly, however, with due regard for the *technological* transformations involved in moving first *from* 'speech' *to* 'writing', both historically and in terms of particular

6   For further elaboration of the relationship between language and technology outlined here, see in particular ch.2 of Bowers (1988), entitled 'Toward a new understanding of technology and language'. See also Hill (1988), especially ch.3 ('Uncovering the technology text').

7   Regarding this matter, see also the chapters by Reid and Christie, in this volume.

individuals' entry into the cultures of schooling and literacy, and then, *between* the two, in the normal course of one's living and learning, in and out of formal educational settings. Once again, technology in and of itself has tended to be an overlooked or underestimated factor in these relationships and transitions, an omission which is becoming more evident as, increasingly, information technology in particular has a direct impact on the cultures and practices of both curriculum and literacy, arguably affecting them considerably.

Indeed, what is extremely interesting in recent accounts of technology is an explicit engagement with language and more specifically the speech/writing relationship, more often than not from a critical perspective which links the media shift from 'speech' to 'writing' with problems in the technological enterprise more generally. For Stephen Hill (1988), for instance, there is clearly a sense of real ambivalence and indeed of significant loss involved in moving from a predominantly oral culture to a written culture, which he presents as essentially a loss in immediacy:

> A culture that is based on written rather than oral texts is quite different to a culture that is based on texts that are actively and orally generated within each moment of life-world experience ... The written text captures only that which can be represented within the grammar and extensiveness of representation that the language allows. So the subjective *experience* of history is not brought into the present in its experiential totality, just those elements that are deemed worthy of written record in a past and different age and culture. (Hill 1988, p.63)

Writing involves not simply *selection*, that is, but also *reduction*, as well as, inevitably in such a view, distortion or even 'misrepresentation'. Significantly, Hill goes on to refer to a direct analogy between technology and writing, as similarly both partial and 'the objectification of cultural values'. He presents an account of technology as 'text', and extends the metaphor of what he calls 'the machine text' in this sense to refer specifically to 'the *machine-text* versions of "written text" ' (Hill 1988, p.71). The whole point of his discussion is that technology re-presents human experience, as does writing, and in doing so transforms it in ways that reduce both its immediacy and its 'meaningfulness'.[8]

A point worth considering is the significance of Hill's choice of metaphor, and the possibility that turning the metaphor back on itself and interrogating its taken-for-granted features from another point of view might be extremely generative for rethinking some of the issues we are concerned with here. This is precisely what Derrida (1976) does, challenging the normative and commonsense view of the speech/writing relationship and arguing for a critical engagement with the concept-metaphor of *enframing*—a term that Hill also uses, albeit somewhat differently ('enframement') and to decidedly different ends. What it draws

---

8   A similar argument can be observed in Carey (1989) and, as he indicates, in Harold Innes (1951), a major although somewhat neglected figure in communications research.

attention to is a complex matter of supplementation and contextualisation, which Derrida contends is intrinsic and crucial to the very idea of technology and similarly of writing. In such an account, the sense of loss associated with writing is revealed as intensely problematical, for one thing because it implies a a pre-cultural, pre-technological state of pure, unmediated being, a mythic moment of original, unsullied presence. Writing and technology alike—writing as technology, and vice versa—can only be 'add-ons', extras, introducing an (un)necessary complexity; rather like the Serpent ...

A argument similar to Hill's, with regard to the negative dimensions of writing and technology, is presented in Bowers (1988), although Bowers focuses more specifically on the cultural consequences of computing and, as indicated previously, 'the non-neutrality of technology'. He links computing directly to literacy and print culture, as opposed to, and indeed as suppressing, orality and its cultural and epistemological concomitants. He sees in the former, increasingly becoming a dominant and determining logic in social life, a significant kind of and predilection towards human *alienation*, understood in terms of 'the separation of the word from the body (the reification of the printed word) and separation in our personal relationships' (Bowers 1988, p.80). As he writes:

> The connection between educational computing and the technological culture of print further supports the arguments that computers are not a neutral technology that simply expand our ability to store and manipulate information. In effect, the privileging of print over orality means that the use of microcomputers strengthens certain cultural patterns and orientations and weakens others. (Bowers 1988, p.83)

It is clear that for Bowers, *despite* the productivity and gains associated with such developments and characteristics of technological development generally—print culture, for instance, fostering and linking up with notions of individual autonomy and analytical thought—there is much to regret in the cultural forms that have emerged so far, in accordance with the logics of technology, and that would seem likely to be strengthened and further consolidated in the future. Part of what is at issue here is a particular notion of *community*, and the need, as Bowers sees it, to work towards an eco-systemic, holistic vision of a distinctively human community, literally grounded in the continued viability of life on Earth. The relationship between computing and literacy, within his frame of reference, is a significant factor in this notion. Hence, there is much to consider, as he argues, with regard to the 'speech/writing' motif in discourse on technology, on a number of levels and in a range of respects.

This is Mark Poster's argument as well, although he works from a completely different perspective, one associated with that 'curious melange of positions known as poststructuralism' (Poster 1990a, p.114). For Poster, at larger issue is the significance of what he calls 'the mode of information', an emergent linguistically oriented form of social organisation, involving new language experiences and 'new language formations that alter significantly the network of social relations, that restructure these relations and the subjects they constitute' (Poster 1990b, p.8). Among the alterations and transformations associated with the new electronic forms of technologically mediated language is that which affects language itself, as well as our understandings of both its nature and its role in social life generally. Traditionally, central to these understandings, as Poster indicates, has been the binary formulation of language in terms of 'speech' and 'writing', associated with which are distinctive 'forms of life'. This formulation has tended to be realised, analytically if not experientially, in terms of the assertion of clearly marked *boundaries*.

However, as he notes, 'the distinction between speech and writing has been gaining attention in the social sciences and the humanities just at the moment when both forms of communication are being overshadowed by electronic media' (Poster 1990a, p.110). Hence, what needs to be stressed is that this strong classification between speech and writing and their associated cultures, epistemologies and forms of life and rationality, increasingly constructed and institutionalised as they are in modernist discourse, is now being radically unsettled. This change has significant implications for the classical notions of *representation* and *subjectivity*, which have hitherto operated as foundational concepts for the various projects of modernity, including normative curriculum and mass schooling. As Poster writes:

> Precisely what characterizes technologically advanced societies in the twentieth centuries is the emergence of new language experiences that are electronically mediated, *fitting into the parameters of neither speech nor writing.* (Poster 1990a, p.113) (my emphasis).

Given this, 'a great deal can be understood about the speech/writing debate if it is contextualized in relation to the emergence of electronic languages' (Poster 1990a, p.113).[9]

Much is at issue, then, in the technological transformation of language experiences, forms and practices. Given the crucial importance of language in education, it is clearly a matter of some urgency that attention be given to the nature, effects and implications of these transformations, and that the relationship between language and technology becomes a priority area of concern for educational theory and practice.

As another instance of the implications of the above arguments for education, consider Lyotard's account of the changing nature and status of *knowledge* as, in his terms, 'societies enter what is known as the postindustrial age and cultures enter what is known as the postmodern

---

9   For elaboration of these issues and this perspective, see Poster (1990b), especially ch.4 ('Derrida and electronic writing'), for specific reference to computers, writing and the poststructuralist concept of subjectivity.

age' (Lyotard 1984, p.3). Noting the particular significance in this regard of new developments in science and technology, and the growing importance of knowledge as both resource and commodity ('indispensable to productive power'—Lyotard 1984, p.5), he observes that such 'technological transformations' as increasingly characterise contemporary societies 'can be expected to have a considerable impact on knowledge' (Lyotard 1984, p.4), and hence on education as the institution specifically oriented and addressed towards its production, transmission and reproduction. Not only does 'knowledge' itself become increasingly problematised as a category, but also it is necessarily changed or transformed—literally—as regards its very nature. Its very nature is changed because it must be rendered into a form amenable to 'the new channels'; that is to say, it can only become 'operational' if '[learning?] is translated into quantities of information'. This raises the question, of course, of which kinds of knowledge are amenable in this regard and in this way, and which are not; and then what are the *educational* implications of what are in effect technologically determined and technologically driven principles of inclusion and exclusion, selection and omission.

A further consideration is what Lyotard describes as 'a thorough exteriorization of knowledge with respect to the "knower", at whatever point he or she may occupy in the knowledge process' (Lyotard 1984, p.4). This point has implications for teachers and students alike, at every level of schooling (including that of the university), in that it changes or at least forces a reconsideration of the general notion of pedagogy. If we understand curriculum as a social practice operating at both the macro and the micro levels of realisation, then the impact of technology—or rather, more specifically, the new information and communications technologies—on curriculum, and hence on schooling, is likely to be of major and perhaps even decisive significance.

At the macro level, we are drawn to reassess the relationship between education and the state, and the manner in which the practices associated with social reproduction and cultural transmission are to be understood. To what extent are the now well-documented functions of education in the generation of inequalities and the consolidation of existing and longstanding forms of cultural, political and economic power actually strengthened as a consequence of computerisation on such a grand scale?

Alternatively, it might be that the securing of 'intergenerational continuity' is in various ways unsettled, interrupted or at least disrupted, as an effect of such transformations. If 'knowledge' is indeed 'exteriorized', as Lyotard puts it, and hence separated from the 'knower', does this mean, at least potentially, that people, especially the young—the new generations— can avoid being drawn into the ambit of official knowledge, given that such knowledge always serves certain socially and culturally dominant interests rather than others and thus is always-already politically charged.

This point leads directly into consideration of what has been previously described as the micro dimensions of curriculum, focused specifically on the notion of student learning, and hence on matters of classroom practice and teachers' work. The question to be addressed here concerns the nature of learning itself, traditionally conceived in terms of 'cognition' and 'mental development'. Learning has always—certainly since Descartes and the Enlightenment—been associated with notions such as 'mind' and 'psyche', and hence with a particular understanding and valorisation of 'interiority' as the primary and perhaps even proper realm of cognition and learning. These notions are linked in turn to a certain normalised and normative view of *rationality*, a view which has become increasingly acknowledged as a problematical category in itself, and indeed as both symptomatic of and instrumental in the privileging of certain perspectives rather than others, particularly along class, gender and ethnocentric lines of social and cultural difference. On the negative side, we can point to the increasing powerlessness—or, more actively, disempowerment—that attends the separation of 'knower' and 'known', bearing in mind once again that this relationship will be very different for different social groupings. What are the principal underlying matters of access and equal opportunity, with regard to changing configurations of power-knowledge? What might 'learning' be, if learners are increasingly dissociated from the new (trans)form(ations)s of knowledge? Indeed, what might 'knowledge' itself be, in the new order of things, detached thus from human beings? This might be something like the classical philosophical problem of the phenomenon of a tree falling in the middle of a forest quite unbeknown to any human knower: can such a phenomenon be said to exist at all? Or is such an analogy at all appropriate in this case, given that some 'humans'—and more pertinently, some social groups—will continue to have a more 'intimate' relationship than others (perhaps the silent majority) with the 'machine', and with the principles and procedures shaping and informing postmodern knowledge of this kind?

More positively, what Lyotard describes as the 'exteriorization of knowledge' can be seen as representing and conducive of changing perspectives on learning and cognition, and even changing forms of learning and cognition. Do we need to think in terms of 'interiority' at all, or of the nature and necessity of 'interiorization', at least exclusively? Might it not be possible to see such technologies as *amplifiers* of human attributes and capacities, and hence of human potential; as prosthetic devices which enable learners to operate differently, and to organise and focus their energies and attention differently?[10] After all, the lament that new technologies of communication and information storage and handling 'externalize' knowledge is hardly new. Plato perceived writing as something that induced 'forgetfulness' and hence reduced the significance of memory as a primary defining feature of both culture and cognition. Later, the invention of the printing press and its associated infrastructure similarly transformed memory and other human attributes, with similar shifts in the nature of and relationship between knowledge and

---

10   Against the notion of 'amplifiers', though, we need to bear in mind that they can also serve as 'atrophiers' ...

subjectivity (Hirst & Woolley 1982). More recently, we need only think of the humble calculator in these terms, and the debates that arose as to whether it reduced students' 'natural' capacity for calculation and other mathematical operations of a supposedly primary (or primal?) nature. And yet, how does a modern device such as the personal electronic calculator differ, substantively, from the premodern abacus?

Conclusion

In conclusion, then, rather than rushing in and presuming that the introduction of the new technologies is *either* positive *or* negative in its educational implication and effect, we need to think very carefully about the range of possibilities and problems that might be associated with them. Only on such a basis can critically informed understandings be matched with prudent actions, educationally and otherwise, whether in our schools or in the larger society. Bearing in mind what has previously been discussed as the 'non-neutrality' thesis and the amplification-reduction dialectic, Ihde is worth quoting once again at this point:

> Together, this amplification-reduction makes a medium nonneutral or transformative of human experience. It is, moreover, a feature of every use of a technology. The term 'nonneutrality' is carefully chosen so as to preclude either some immediate 'good' or equally immediate 'bad' connotation for technologies. It is, rather, essentially or invariably ambiguous, and this inescapable ambiguity makes the use and development of technologies simultaneously fascinating, threatening, and in need of serious reflection. (Ihde 1982, p.64)

It is this notion of 'ambiguity' that I want especially to emphasise here, although it might be equally appropriate to express it as 'ambivalence' or indeed as 'contradictoriness'. The point is, however, to draw attention to what is certainly a crucial feature of technology, understood in the broadest sense and hence as including what can be described as the technological imagination—its complexly ambiguous, ambivalent and contradictory nature—and the need, accordingly, for a theory and politics of technology that is equally complex, whether it be in social life and the realm of cultural practice more generally or more specifically in relation to education.

References

Bowers, C. (1988), *The Cultural Dimensions of Educational Computing: Understanding the Non-neutrality of Technology*, Teachers College Press, New York.

Carey, J.W. (1989), 'Technology and ideology: The case of the telegraph', in J.W. Carey, *Communication as Culture: Essays on Media and Society*, Unwin Hyman, Boston, Mass.

Carey, J.W. with Quirk, J.J. (1989), 'The mythos of the electronic revolution', in J.W. Carey, *Communication as Culture: Essays on Media and Society*, Unwin Hyman, Boston, Mass.

Chambers, I. (1986), 'Waiting on the end of the world?', *Journal of Communication Inquiry*, vol.10, no.2, pp.99–107.

de Lauretis, T., Huyssen, A. & Woodward, K. (eds) (1980), *The Technological Imagination: Theories and Fictions*, Coda Press, Madison, Wis.

Derrida, J. (1976), *Of Grammatology*, trans. G.C. Spivak, Johns Hopkins University Press, Baltimore, Md.

Derrida, J. (1978), *Writing and Difference*, trans. A. Bass, Routledge & Kegan Paul, London.

Donald, J. (1983), 'How illiteracy became a problem (and literacy stopped being one)', *Journal of Education*, vol.165, no.1, pp.35–52.

During, S. (1987), 'Postmodernism or post-colonialism today?', in A. Milner, P. Thompson & C. North (eds), *Postmodern Conditions*, Berg Publishers, New York.

Featherstone,M. (1988), 'In pursuit of the postmodern: An introduction', *Theory, Culture and Society*, vol.5, nos 2–3, pp.195–215.

Giroux, H.A. (1990), *Curriculum Discourse as Postmodernist Critical Practice*, ECS802 Curriculum Theory, Deakin University, Geelong, Vic.

Green, B. (ed.) (1993), *The Insistence of the Letter: Literacy Studies and Curriculum Theorizing*, Falmer Press, London.

Haraway, D.J. (1991), *Simians, Cyborgs, and Women: The Reinvention of Nature*, Routledge, New York.

Hayles, N.K. (1990), *Chaos Bound: Orderly Disorder in Contemporary Literature and Science*, Cornell University Press, Ithaca, NY.

Hill, S. (1988), *The Tragedy of Technology: Human Liberation versus Domination in the Late Twentieth Century*, Pluto Press, London.

Hinkson, J. (1987), 'Post-Lyotard: A critique of the information society', *Arena*, no.80, pp.123–55.

Hirst P. & Woolley, P. (1982), *Social Relations and Human Attributes*, Tavistock Publications, London.

Hunter, I. (1984), 'After representation: Recent discussions of the relation between language and literature', *Economy and Society*, vol.13, no.1, pp.397–403.

Ihde, D. (1982), 'The technological embodiment of media', in M.J. Hyde (ed.), *Communication, Philosophy and the Technological Age*, University of Alabama Press, Tuscaloosa.

Ihde, D. (1990), *Technology and the Lifeworld: From Garden to Earth*, Indiana University Press, Bloomington.

Innes, H. (1951), *The Bias of Communication*, Toronto University Press, Toronto.

Jameson F. (1984), 'Postmodernism, or the cultural logic of late capitalism', *New Left Review*, no.146, pp.53–92

Jenkins, E. (1988), School Writing, Technologies, and Textuality, Honours dissertation, School of Education, Murdoch University, WA.

Lankshear, C. with Lawler, M. (1987), *Literacy, Schooling and Revolution*, Falmer Press, New York.

Lather, P. (1991), *Getting Smart: Feminist Research and Pedagogy within/in the Postmodern*, Routledge, New York.

Luke, A. (1988), *Literacy, Textbooks and Ideology: Postwar Literacy Instruction and the Mythology of Dick and Jane*, Falmer Press, London.

Lyotard, J.-F. (1984), *The Postmodern Condition: A Report on Knowledge*, trans. G. Bennington & B. Massumi, University of Minnesota Press, Minneapolis.

Merchant, C. (1980), *The Death of Nature: Women, Ecology and the Scientific Revolution*, Harper & Row, New York.

Monaghan, E.J. & Saul, E.W. (1987), 'The reader, the scribe, the thinker: A critical look at the history of American reading and writing instruction', in T.S. Popkewitz (ed.), *The Formation of the School Subjects: The Struggle for Creating an American Institution*, Falmer Press, New York.

Nichols, B. (1988), 'The work of culture in the age of cybernetic systems', *Screen*, vol.29, no.1, pp.22–46.

Poster, M. (1990a), 'Foucault and data bases', *Discourse*, vol.12, no.2, pp.110–27.

Poster, M. (1990b), *The Mode of Information: Poststructuralism and Social Context*, Polity Press, London.

Scribner, S. & Cole, M. (1981), *The Psychology of Literacy*, Harvard University Press, Cambridge, Mass.

Ulmer, G.L. (1985), *Applied Grammatology: Post(e)-Pedagogy from Jacques Derrida to Joseph Beuys*, Johns Hopkins University Press, Baltimore, Md.

Virilio, P. (1989), *War and Cinema: The Logistics of Perception*, trans. P. Camiller, Verso, London.

Part I

Part I

Curriculum as text

Stephen Kemmis

We frequently think of curricula as 'transmitting' what students need to know, as if they could—in some unproblematical sense—represent the world to rising generations. In this chapter, I want to treat this idea of 'representation' as problematic. Unfortunately (to anticipate my conclusion), I have no advice to give on how to escape the obligation to represent the world to rising generations through the curriculum, even though representation must mean something much more complex than a copy theory of meaning might suggest—the theory that meanings or texts can somehow provide a 'copy' of the way the world is. So, we are confronted with a paradox: how to represent the world to rising generations when representation is not the kind of practice which allows a secure or certain knowledge and control of the world or how it can be understood.

In the first section of this chapter, I refer to a number of novels—some from early this century and others more recent—to show how their authors have played with our readerly expectations of what a story is and how it can be told. I use this exploration to suggest that in developing curricula we are writing and presenting stories, and that we should be aware of the tenuousness and complexity of the relationship between authors, texts and readers. Sometimes we think of curricula as 'maps' to society and culture; my romp through some of the good reads I have had lately convinces me that the metaphor of the map is inadequate in understanding what curricula are and how they work. I then explore one or two other metaphors suggested by two contemporary novelists. This exploration provides a basis for suggesting a range of connections to be taken into account in understanding how a curriculum works in relation to its setting and society. Given what I have said about the metaphor of maps, I cannot suggest that the analytical scheme I present is a 'map' of the field of curriculum, but maybe it can present (is that just a way of avoiding saying 're-present'?) a way of thinking about curriculum.

What this chapter aims to achieve, then, is not so much the presentation of a reliable view of curricula as 'texts', but a problematisation of the idea of 'representation'. As teachers, we are always trapped in a paradoxical situation in which, on the one hand, we want to tell our students what the world (or some aspect of it) is like—to represent the world to them—while, on the other, we know that our representations of the world are always frail and artificial. It may not be much of an achievement to convince you that we must learn to live with the uncertainty this paradox creates; on the other hand, if I succeed in undermining the view that a curriculum can represent the world in an unproblematic way, the chapter will have served its purpose.

Authors, texts and readers

I can still smile with pleasure when I recall my first encounter with Erich Auerbach's *Mimesis*, an analysis of the representation of reality in literature. I well remember bobbing in the stream of Auerbach's text, jostling with the flotsam of textual fragments selected more or less at random from the literature of two millennia, and beginning to understand what Auerbach so clearly demonstrated: that, in quite historically specific ways, authors call on readers' own social experience to give a sense of reality to characters constructed in imagination. Auerbach shows how Homer gave his characters identity by speaking of them as descendants of parents and grandparents, for example, and how Virginia Woolf gave characters a humanity by having them measured for new clothes, as if catching them unawares in fleeting and intimate domestic moments. As readers, we must be given clues which link the lives and identities of characters to our own ways of knowing ourselves.

If I recall correctly, Auerbach's last fragment is drawn from Virginia Woolf's *To the Lighthouse,* first published on 5 May 1927. The 1920s were heady times for the novel. Readers were being challenged in unexpected ways, being forced to learn very new ways of reading. Consider, for example, the shock experienced by the first readers of James Joyce's *Ulysses*, published in Paris on Joyce's fortieth birthday, 2 February 1922. And the shocks have kept coming as the novel has continued to evolve during the twentieth century, making new and varied assaults on our capacity to believe and to suspend disbelief, and teaching us, as readers, new forms of distrust for the authorial voice of the novelist.

Lawrence Durrell's 'Alexandria Quartet', for example, treats readers to a series of novels which overlap and intertwine, each revealing new perspectives on previous stories and showing each to be partial and incomplete just where it seemed to be most conclusive and complete. In the first, *Justine* (1956), a young man recounts his perplexing experiences in an affair in Alexandria, only to find that he has misunderstood much of what was going on around him—as is revealed in *Balthazar* (1958), the second of the quartet, when his old friend Balthazar, in a great 'interlinear', tells him something of what was between or behind the lines of the first narrative. The third novel in the quartet, *Mountolive* (1958), is an apparently innocent and more traditional narrative, sitting more or less alongside the events of the first two, but further compounding and ramifying the earlier ones by refracting many of the same characters and events in still different ways. The fourth novel, *Clea* (1960), is an almost conventional sequel in which the central characters are taken into yet new sets of interrelationship. Here we have a novelist leaving spaces between his lines which he later explores, revealing the partiality of earlier views. Clearly, the narrative 'I' of the novels does not know all; there is always more to know, and the 'gaps' in the imaginary world Durrell creates reveals at least that the narrative 'I' (of the novels) and the author are separate people with different knowledge, which is always limited, partial, and open to expansion and correction.

In the 'Alexandria Quartet', the partiality and incompleteness of each of the separate novels suggests that, with more complete information, a more comprehensive picture or narrative might be possible. Individual perspectives might be incomplete, but perhaps a more omniscient author or narrator might put this unitary whole together.

With Durrell's 'Avignon' quincunx of novels (*Monsieur*, 1974; *Livia*, 1978; *Constance*, 1982; *Sebastian*, 1983; *Quinx*, 1985), things became even more complex: five interrelated texts reflect and refract one another's central themes and characters. Key themes and relationships are established, then subjected to almost mathematical transformation. With formal precision, the author conducts a literary experiment which includes the manufacture of a range of linked characters including at least two authors who seem to be, in turn, creating one another, and, along with them, a range of others whose identities and relationships are formed, deformed and transformed from book to book. In the 'Avignon' novels, the paradoxical possibility of the more comprehensive story seems to have been eliminated: realities are more clearly dependent on perspective, and transformations of perspective are seen to 'produce' different effects: different stories. By now, the hand that holds the authorial pen has become so intrusive as to suggest a new level of realism. The quincunx seems to beg the reader to enquire into the author himself: what is the experience and what are the preoccupations of the man conducting this grand experiment? But is this the 'real' Lawrence Durrell, or is the experimenting novelist just another authorial mask?

The games authors play have become even more extravagant in magical-realist novels like Italo Calvino's *If on a Winter's Night a Traveller*, Gabriel Garcia Marquez's *One Hundred Years of Solitude* and *Love in the Time of Cholera*, Mario Vargas Llosa's *Aunt Julia and the Scriptwriter*, Isabel Allende's *House of Spirits* and Salman Rushdie's *Midnight's Children*. All conjure with our readerly expectations and invite us to accept premises from which anything at all might follow—yet still persuading us that truths worth telling can be told through such fiction. Here authors are explicitly on display, sometimes as fictive narrators, sometimes as characters who actually bear the authors' own names. The gap between the author as private person and public persona arrestingly described by Jorge Luis Borges in his 'Borges and I' (in Borges' *A Personal Anthology*) is changed when an author like Calvino makes a character of 'himself'.

Not only authors but also the texts themselves have become slippery. They make magical mixtures of the real, the possible, the improbable, the impossible and the fantastic. We are no longer invited to suspend disbelief but to play with it. We are invited to test the 'truth' (?) that the truth about ourselves and the world can only be told through fiction. What kinds of truths can these be? And, as if this were not enough, such texts may even 'instruct' us in reading, with Calvino going so far (in *If on a Winter's Night a Traveller*) as to help us arrange ourselves comfortably in our chairs to read what may or may not be the novel we wanted to read—a novel about a reader (and an author) in search of a novel.

In these newish novels, the author, the reader and the text are explicitly conceived and considered as trapped in a common web, woven deliberately to show how the ensnarement of imagination is achieved in textual practices—practices of writing and of reading, and the intertextual construction of whole genres of texts. Mark Henshaw's first novel, *Out of the Line of Fire*, begins with the opening lines of Italo Calvino's *If on a Winter's Night a Traveller*, explicitly locating its own text in relation to Calvino's and urging the reader to bring to mind Calvino's experiments with authorship and readership.

The all-knowing, magisterial voice of the author is a thing of the past; the imaginary worlds of these novels are no longer to be evaluated against their correspondence with the 'realities' readers know, but against the poetic possibilities of transformed worlds which seem unreal, quite different from the banalities of readers' everyday existence. Readers are invited to join a game of imagination in which the ordered surfaces of the world are surprisingly deformed and reformed, deconstructed and reconstructed in a wordplay which forces us to reconsider our ways of interpreting the world and to see it as manifold and multiple rather than as a unified and unitary whole. Not only do these novels teach us much about authors, texts and readers; they also tell us about the problems of telling any story—problems of the creation and interpretation of texts which science (including educational science) also shares.

Georges Perec, in *Life: A User's Manual*, has constructed a novel (if it can properly be called that) which billows out in a web of connections from a Paris apartment house. One resident spends twenty years travelling to ports around the world where he paints watercolours which are then turned into jigsaw puzzles which he then spends the rest of his life reassembling, and having them reglued so the pictures can be stripped off the wooden backing and returned to the places where they were painted to be washed out, reducing the paper to its initial condition. Another resident is a painter who wants to paint 179 scenes depicting objects and moments in the life of the apartment house and its residents. There is a suspicion that the book might be these pictures put into words. Each chapter is a minutely detailed scene (as it might be perceived from the perspective of someone who 'reads' each scene as if it were a piece of a jigsaw puzzle, wondering how it fits with the other pieces). Details of newspapers, books, labels, items found on the stairs, biscuit tins, paintings and other objects are examined and reported in a way little different from the mode Perec adopts in describing the people and events in the still-life scenes of the book. A substantial index cross-references residents, objects, authors, streets and historical figures; a chronology offers a crude historical frame (like the white border of the jigsaw?), as does a crude map of the apartment building; an alphabetical checklist of some of the tales reported in the book provides a way of approaching its lessons from 'life', even if one must have read the book to make conjectures about what the morals from these tales might be. And even if Perec's pieces can be made to fit together as a single 'jigsaw', there seem to be pieces missing; in any case, the 'story' told in the jigsaw seems as arbitrarily chosen as the picture which is the basis for any jigsaw—as if it were no more than a better or worse excuse for a puzzle and for puzzling?

In Milorad Pavic's 'lexicon novel', *Dictionary of the Khazar,*[1] the relationship between the writer and the reader is adumbrated:

> As for you, the writer, never forget the following: the reader is like a circus horse which has to be taught that it will be rewarded with a lump of sugar every time it acquits itself well. If that sugar is withheld, it will not perform. As for essayists and critics, they are like cuckolded husbands: always the last to find out ... (Pavic 1989, p.15)

Few books test the reader's capacity to perform like a circus horse quite so thoroughly as the *Dictionary of the Khazars,* which requires a strenuous leaping back and forth between separate alphabeticised Hebrew, Islamic and Christian compilations of information (laced with competing misinformation and disinformation) about the Khazars, their (Jewish, Muslim and Greek) chroniclers and the (Jewish, Muslim and Greek) scholars who have studied them. The relationship between writer, reader and text is more completely explained in the following helpful image:

> Imagine two men holding a captured puma on a rope. If they want to approach each other, the puma will attack, because the rope will slacken; only if they both pull simultaneously on the rope is the puma equidistant from the two of them. That is why it is so hard for him who reads and him who writes to reach each other: between them lies a mutual thought captured on ropes that they pull in opposite directions. If we were now to ask that puma—in other words, that thought—how it perceived these two men, it might answer that at the ends of the rope those to be eaten are holding someone they cannot eat ... (Pavic 1989, p.14)

By now, we readers have learned a thing or two. We have learned that authors may or may not be who they say they are, or appear to be; that

---

1   Hamish Hamilton, London, 1989, translated from the Serbo-Croatian by Christina Pribicevic-Zoric. Note that the quotations reproduced here are from the 'Female Edition' of the dictionary. My copy clearly states: 'The Male Edition is almost identical. But NOT quite. Be warned that ONE PARAGRAPH is crucially different'. One of these quotations could be from the paragraph in question. In the two following quotations, by the way, authors and readers are both referred to using the male pronoun. Could this be sexist language, and, if so, was it perhaps introduced at the point of translation by the (female) translator? Or is this a deliberate feature of the 'Female Edition'? Is the 'Female Edition' intended for male or female readers? Or is its gender somehow intrinsic to the text itself?

what texts express is not necessarily what they seem to say, or what they say they are saying; and that we are constructed as readers by authors who teach us to be readers by the tasks they set us, as well as by the reading tasks we set ourselves (and that our friends set us) in choosing and reading books. In *If on a Winter's Night a Traveller*, Italo Calvino reminds us of how we are led to reading by our choices in buying books (the ones we feel we ought to read, the ones we want to put beside others on our shelves, the ones we already know without reading them, and so on). Milorad Pavic is even more blunt: he tells us that, even having started the book, we can, perhaps should, turn back:

> The author advises the reader not to tackle this book unless he absolutely has to. And if he does touch it, let it be on days when he feels that his mind and sense of caution probe deeper than usual, and let him read it the way he catches 'leap-fever', an illness that skips over every other day and strikes only on feminine days of the week. (Pavic 1989, p.14)

Like a good circus horse, I did not turn back. I performed for my sugar, persisting even when it tasted fishy. And all this says something about textual practice, I suppose, though I am not sure it is the kind of practice that makes perfect.

Curriculum as carpet and map ...

In *Invisible Cities*, Italo Calvino has Marco Polo tell the story of Eudoxia, a rambling, convoluted city in which there is a carpet which, the inhabitants say, provides a map of the city and the lives of all those who live in it. When lost, people can always find themselves and their way by referring to the pattern of the carpet. An oracle says that the correspondence between these two dissimilar objects, the city and the carpet, is explained by the fact that one is divinely inspired. It is supposed that it is the carpet that is of divine origin, but Polo (or Calvino) wonders whether it might not be the city itself which is divinely inspired, and the carpet the fallible, faulty human creation.

Curricula are sometimes described as maps of the social realities they intend to represent. But they are also very fallible human creations. At best, they may be no more than inadequate representations; at worst, they may give only the illusion that they represent, in the way that the carpet may have no more than an illusory relation with the city of Eudoxia.

Drawing on a tradition of textual authority going back to the recitation of sacred texts, we have learned to make, read and practise curricula as if they were maps. Because the interpretation of sacred texts was once premised on the possibility of arriving at a correct interpretation of the word of God, perhaps we still share a vestige of the belief that true knowledge can be attained in the interpretation of an authoritative text, and a vestige of the belief that authoritative texts can point us to certainties about how things really are, though nowadays scientific texts have usurped the authority once associated with religious texts. Even though we may mistrust their simplifications, we retain the charming hope that curriculum texts are (or should be, or can be) in some sense reliable. As texts (practised in writing, reading and being performed), they may be more or less adequate representations of a society for rising generations, but they are almost always inspired by the will to represent. By the last part of the twentieth century, we are inclined to take it for granted that they have this fundamental pedagogical purpose. In fact, the 'mapping' involved in curriculum is a double mapping, a double task of representing. We believe that curricula are capable both of guiding students in their action in the world and of guiding teachers in their work of representing the world to rising generations.

I want to argue, however, that curricula are not just like maps. Just as we ask whether the city or the carpet is divinely inspired in the story of Eudoxia, we must ask whether the curriculum or the society it aims to represent is the touchstone for education— especially since we know both to be historically, socially and all-too-humanly constructed. The map metaphor turns out to be only a very alluring simplification: there is a tension between curriculum makers and teachers and students (and others) which the map metaphor cannot capture.

In another of Calvino's 'invisible cities', the inhabitants carry different coloured threads with them as they move from place to place, leaving a record of their movements and their purposes. Perhaps this is another kind of map that we would like a curriculum to be: something which captured all the movements and the purposes of our society. But perhaps not: Calvino's Marco Polo tells the Great Khan that after a time, this city becomes entangled and ensnared in the threads, so the inhabitants must abandon it and find a new location, starting again. The 'map' created by the threads describes a city that is now dead; the inhabitants can no longer endure living in the tangle of its history. Curricula are a bit like that, too, one might think.

Curricula are also a bit like the puma's of Pavic's story: that which cannot be eaten held in place on ropes between those (teachers, students) it can eat. Of course the metaphor of the puma on the ropes also simplifies too much: there are many 'authors', many 'readers' and many 'pumas' to consider in the making and using of curricula: teachers, texts and students are held in an intricate web of ropes. And behind the teachers who make and use curricula stretch ropes to others (like curriculum developers in education departments and ministries, and the writers of textbooks) who are also involved in their making, and to still others who form the genre of texts we call curricula. And behind the students who 'read' these curriculum 'texts' stretch ropes to their families and to others (such as employers and communities) who shape and sometimes share expectations about what it is to learn, to be schooled, to be educated.

In this image, the ropes symbolise the dynamic tension of being in social relationships. Like all images, this one is acceptable as far as it goes. But there is more: the ropes that link writers and readers and users of curricula are themselves constructed; they are constituted out of the social practices which daily make and remake the relationships between people. And these are not intangibles; they are not invisible threads. For the moment, we might say that they are material practices: they are things done by people, in which relations between people and objects are expressed in transformations of both the people and the objects of their activity. Such material social practices include at least the three commonplace social practices (or modes of interaction) of *communication, production* and *social organisation,* and (probably always) all three in intertwined and interdependent patterns.

These interconnections are very complex indeed. They cannot be represented in any simple 'model' of curriculum or curriculum development (any more than the world and its societies can be simply represented by a curriculum). And there, perhaps, I should stop, lest going further with an analysis of these things may be to start to build a model or a map of curriculum making. Yet, for educators and for societies, it seems to me, there is no alternative to trying to represent the world to rising generations, and for theorists and practitioners of curriculum, there is no alternative to trying to represent and understand our curriculum work. So now we must approach the puma. Carefully.

In what follows, I will proceed in a series of steps to show something of the complexity of the interconnections created in the material social practices of communication, production and social organisation in education. (This task of deconstruction leads us, along another route, to the perspective expressed by the central character in Salman Rushdie's *Midnight's Children:* 'To understand just one person, you must understand the whole world. I told you that'.)

Interconnections
When we look at classrooms (as when we look at most other social settings), we can always see three kinds of things happening:

• people talking: expressing and interpreting meanings, and explaining and justifying what they do; that is, *communication;*

• people working: doing things with things to make other, transformed, things through their labour; that is, *production*; and

• people arranging and rearranging their activities to coordinate with one another in groups, involving them in conflict and consensus, control and resistance; that is, *organisation.*

Each of these modes of activity involves characteristic 'genres', one might say: each occurs in a distinctive *social medium.* Respectively, communication, production and social organisation occur in the distinctive and interrelated, though also familiar, forms and patterns of *language, work* and *power.* To understanding how language, work and power shape our lives is to understand a story rather like that of the selfish gene: in the process of evolution, do species use genes to reproduce themselves, or is it the genes that reproduce and develop themselves through species? Sometimes we are blinded by the images of ourselves as *users* of language, work and power. Self-importantly, we think of these things as tools for our use, as 'for us'. We might also say that we are objects (or is it subjects?) 'for them'. Historically speaking, human beings have constituted (and continue to constitute and reconstitute) these media for our use, but we also constitute ourselves through them and in them. Thus, we might say:

- I speak language, but my language also 'speaks' me: it gives me the possibility of meaning, of saying something new by the use of its familiar tokens.

- I work for a living, but my work also shapes my life.

- I relate to others (in structures of power), but my relationships also give me my social identity.

These circles of constitution and reconstitution are at the heart of the social construction of reality—and the social construction of ourselves.

The familiar patterns of language, work and power are not simply generated by agreement among those participating in the immediate setting of their interaction. They are shaped (historically and socially constructed) in much broader contexts of social life and tradition: they are shaped by *social structures*. They have a historical existence as practices across settings, linking one setting to another, linking people to each other within and across settings, and (one might say) developing and evolving as social media in their own right, almost as 'objects' which have their own existence independently of individual actors:

- Communication through *language* develops and evolves across historically formed and formative contexts of *culture*.

- Production through *work* develops and evolves across historically formed and formative contexts of *economic activity*.

- Organisation through the exercise of *power* develops and evolves across historically formed and formative contexts of *political life*.

The main structural characteristics of societies (social structures) can be described, somewhat statically, in terms of the history and substance of the patterns and traditions of cultural life, economic life and political life which constitute them, and, more dynamically, by reference to characteristic constituting social practices of communication, production and organisation.

Through these constituting structures and practices, the *knowledge* of individuals is also formed:

- the *understandings and meanings* which people learn and develop through communication in language in a wider cultural context;

- the *skills* which people learn and develop through participating in production in a wider economic context; and

- the *values and social orientations* which people learn and develop through organising and being organised in a wider political context.

Just as communication, production and social organisation are always intertwined, so understandings, skills and values are interdependent; they are learned and developed in the context of one another. In the same way, culture, economy and politics are interdependent in society; as are forms and patterns of language, work and power. The 'texts' of communication (written or spoken, read or heard, as well as those of an audio-visual nature) always occur in contexts of production and organisation; 'texts' of production always occur in contexts of communication and organisation; 'texts' of organisation always occur in contexts of communication and production. And these 'texts' always occur in contexts of culture, economy and politics. And they always depend on the coding and decoding of meanings, the exercise of skills, and participation in social relationships.

My point here is that knowledge is not just in heads, it is also embodied and made tangible in material practices and media (texts) which 'connect' people to one another. The forms these texts take are constructed and reconstructed in use and by users, and they are formative of their users and the uses to which they may be put. They have, simultaneously, a 'givenness' (their conservation across settings and people) and a malleability and adaptability that allows them to be transformed and reconstituted in new settings of use and new uses.

When all this is put in the context of education, and its individual and social functions which include (at the two levels of individual knowledge and social structure) both the *reproduction* and the *transformation* of knowledge and forms of social life, this set of relationships may be summarised as in Table 1.

Especially since the rise of mass schooling in the late nineteenth century, schools have intervened in the broad processes of social reproduction and transformation systematically to supplement learning by doing in family, economic and community life with specially designed opportunities for learning in distinctive, purpose-built social settings (schools and classrooms) which were constructed to give rising generations access to the increasingly complex structures of industrial society. Societies could no longer be regarded as self-disclosing; students could no longer be expected to understand the world around them unaided. Mass schooling was created to give students a kind of overview of society—albeit imperfect and limited—which would show them ways to 'fit in' to the social life of the industrial states of the late nineteenth century. At this time even more than in earlier times, the work of schooling was (and it still is) the reproduction and transformation of individual knowledge and social life, but mass schooling brought these processes to a new level of rationalism in planning and provision: it aimed to construct a new generation fitted for life in the new industrial economies and the new civic forms of nation states.

Table 1
Initial theoretical framework

Education involves the reproduction and transformation of		The processes of development and change involved are expressed in contestation and institutionalism in		
Individual (identity and agency) ↗ ↘	Knowledge ⧺	Understandings	Skills	Values
	Social practices (modes of interaction) ⧺	Communication	Production (& consumption)	Organisation
Society (ideology and structure) ↗ ↘	Social structure ⧺	Culture	Economy	Political life
	Social media ⧺	Language	Work	Power

The form and content of *classroom life*—its patterns of communication, production and organisation—can be 'read' in the forms and content of the *curriculum,* the forms and patterns of *pedagogy,* and the forms and patterns of classroom *authority*. In different ways, each of these was constructed to represent the wider social world in which students lived. A kind of correspondence between the life of schooling and the forms of cultural, economic, and family, community and civic life was assumed. Schooling aimed to inculcate new 'scientific' ways of seeing the world; language, literacy and numeracy skills for an emerging white-collar workforce and for the moral improvement of all; obedience, punctuality and patriotism. In such ways, schools were designed to prepare rising generations for adult life; to some extent, they replaced participation in adult life with participation in a kind of artificial, beginners' version of adult life. There was a real aspiration to make schools a kind of microcosm of society. As we now know, the 'microcosm' turned out to be a startlingly distorted one—one which tells a great deal about the vision, perspectives and interests of the educational policy makers, administrators, teachers and others who created it. For example, the content of curricula and recommended pedagogies tell us much about their makers' assumptions about gender, class and ability.

To summarise, the mediation between individual and society through classroom communication, production and organisation may thus be 'read' in:

School and classroom in their	Curriculum content	Pedagogy	Authority and organisation

With the rise of mass schooling, it was not just schools that burgeoned. They were constructed in whole systems designed to provide, regulate and control the work of schooling. Well before the rise of mass schooling, the church, guilds and the state had provided the organisational and administrative machinery for governing education; with the rise of mass schooling, this administrative apparatus was extended. Throughout this century, there has been a massive elaboration of the machinery by which schools are provided, resourced, regulated and controlled. There has been such an elaboration of systems that they now involve complex and diffuse divisions of labour among workers within state education systems. The machinery of *educational administration* has now become so complex that it, in turn, requires regulation. This regulation has been achieved by increasing control of *educational policy, administrative work practices and procedures,* and (usually hierarchical and bureaucratic) *system structures.* A new level of mediation has been added to the mediation between individual and society within schools: the mediation of relationships between individual education workers and society (both in system structures and in wider community relationships).

With the rise of mass schooling, then, the educational functions of individual and social reproduction and transformation are thus subject to a double mediation: once at the level of the school (for teachers and students) and again at the level of education systems (permitting control of the work of students, teachers, school administrators and system-level administrators). This second level of mediation may be summarised in terms of practices of communication, production and organisation in:

Educational administration in its	Educational policy	Administrative work practices and procedures	System structures

To depict these two levels of mediation characteristic of contemporary schooling, we may include them in the initial framework outlined in Table 1 to produce a rough overall theoretical framework as depicted in Table 2.

One might use these categories in the analysis of curriculum practice in a school or classroom setting to tease out these relationships in the particular setting (for example, attempting to see how individuals' understandings, skills and values were related to their participation in structured patterns of (school and classroom) communication, production and organisation, and to try to discover how these structured patterns are related to wider social structures of the culture, economy and political life, as expressed in the social media of language, work and power). The relationships are not just vertical in this framework, however; they are also

46

horizontal and diagonal, with each cell in the matrix being structured in relation to the others.

Table 2
General theoretical framework

Education involves the reproduction and transformation of		The processes of development and change involved are expressed in contestation and institutionalism in		
Individual (identity and agency) ↗ ↘	Knowledge	⧧Understandings	Skills	Values
	Social practices (modes of interaction)	⧧Communication	Production (& consumption)	Organisation
In mass schooling, mediated ↗ ↘	in schools and classrooms by →	Curriculum content	Pedagogy	Authority and organisation
	in educational administration by →	Educational policy	Administrative work practices and procedures	System structures
Society (ideology and structure) ↗ ↘	Social structure	⧧Culture	Economy	Political life
	Social media	⧧Language	Work	Power

Starting with classroom patterns (curriculum content, pedagogy, and authority and organisation), one might work 'outwards' to more general social structures through administrative structures (educational policy, administrative work practices and procedures, and system structures), but general social structures (like cultural, economic and political structures) also exert their effects directly through all of us as persons and citizens, not just through the roles we may take as teachers or students or parents. We are not just determined by our 'official' roles and positions, but also by the historical and social forces that shape and construct us as people (of a certain gender, class, or cultural background, for example): that is, we are shaped by wider community connections and social movements, as well as through the formal structures of the state and the social order. We are also ideologically shaped by the possibilities (and silences and constraints) structured into the social media of language, work and power (and of course we shape the social world and the others with whom we interact through the ways we express ourselves in all of these media) in very general ways which are not limited to the particular social structures we happen to find ourselves in (that is, these media exert general effects across specific culturally, economically and politically structured settings with their specific patterns of communication, production—and consumption—and organisation).

The theoretical framework this set of categories provides is forced and unsatisfactory if applied mechanically to any particular curriculum setting in which we might find ourselves. It is not a 'map', though maybe it indicates something of the 'ropes' of interconnection between some of the aspects of education and social life which need to be considered in thinking about the curriculum. It is better regarded as a 'table of invention'—a set of possible connections to be explored in thinking about curriculum matters. It does no more than suggest possible linkages. For example, by working from the contents and forms of classroom communication, production and organisation, we can explore their relationships with the knowledge being taught and learned in the classroom (understandings, skills and values) on the one hand, and with social structures and media on the other (cultural forms, economic forms and political forms and the ways they are expressed in language, work and power relations). Exploring connections and contradictions within and between the cells in the table can generate critical insights about education, schooling, curriculum and educational administration which suggest new possibilities for curriculum action.

Maps, ropes and webs
Just imagine: around the world, in thousands of different classrooms in thousands of different societies, thousands of different teachers teach a topic like multiplication to thousands of different groups of students, speaking hundreds of different languages, though some common ideas recur across at least some of these multifarious sites. In some sense, they are all teaching something different, and in another sense, they are all teaching the same thing: multiplication. And each student is learning the same thing and, at the same time, something different.

Just imagine: teachers in ten thousand Australian schools are all doing the same (or is it?) thing: preparing the rising generation for adult participation in Australian society. To what extent do they interpret this task in the same way? To what extent do they interpret 'Australian society' in the same way? The 'thing' they aim to represent (Australian society) is only brought into being as an entity through interpretation. Does not each school, each teacher—each student, even—create an idiosyncratic image of what it is, what its basic elements are, and how they are composed in some unifying arrangement? There is no 'real' Australia— 'Australia Unobserved'. Whether or not such an entity exists cannot be decided, because the 'Australia' that exists exists only in the eye of an observer. There is only 'Australia Observed' which is, of course, some version of 'Australia Interpreted'. Because there are so many observer-interpreters of 'Australia', there are many, many 'Australia Observeds'. Yet there are some elements of what 'Australia' is that are common to a number of accounts of what 'Australia' is, some elements which are common to many accounts, and some elements which reveal the unique and idiosyncratic perspectives of particular observers.

One source of the differences in interpretation of Australian society is tradition. There are many different traditions of observing and interpreting 'Australia' (though these traditions are themselves also differently observed and interpreted). One seeks what is uniquely 'Australia' by emphasising geology, another by emphasising geography (the tyranny of distance?), another by emphasising a unique multicultural

48

blend, another by emphasising economic exchanges, another by emphasising constitutional structures, and so on.

This is at the heart of the curriculum problem understood as a problem of representation: what is the signified (the 'real' Australia?) and what is the signifier (the word or concept 'Australia'), and how is each constituted except in traditions and practices of signification—traditions and practices of representation which are starkly revealed in the content of school curricula? The active life of these traditions can be traced through the history of school curricula—a confused debris of historically changing representations left behind, like flotsam left on the beach by the receding tide. Are the earlier images less accurate or adequate than the later ones, or are they merely less interpretable from the perspective of present observers? What 'Australia' is and means has changed as its observers and interpreters have changed, and the succession of interpretations may or may not be progress towards something which is more essentially or more comprehensively 'Australia'. From the history of school curricula, we can see that *what is regarded as* 'Australia' changes, with history, evolution, and the accretions and attritions of passing time.

When we hold this imaginary object 'Australia' firmly in view, we may begin to form the view that it is a unity which has undergone, and continues to undergo, transformations: it is and has always been in the process of becoming something else. When do the sharp breaks in this process occur? With the shifts of tectonic plates that break an island continent off from other continents? With the eruption from the land of the Aboriginal spirit ancestors? With white settlement? With federation? And what remains constant across the changes? Not the continent's edges, nor the population, nor the constitution. How much of what we see of 'Australia' is what it is itself, and how much of 'Australia' is what we can say about it? And how much of 'Australia' is what we want to impress upon others about it (especially the young)? How much is true, good or glorious, and how much false, bad and ignominious?

Within such webs we weave not just 'Australia' but also 'ourselves'. We weave images to present to these teachers and students, at this time, for this or that particular purpose. We reveal our own preoccupations in the way we locate and orient those teachers and students in Australian society.

Earlier, I suggested that the metaphor of the map was very limited as a way of thinking about curriculum. It depends on a notion of representation that suggests that the world has a unified and unitary character that can somehow be faithfully represented to rising generations. The notion that the curriculum is a 'text' is powerful, but in the opening pages of this chapter I suggested that we can no longer regard authors, texts or even readers as we once did: as many contemporary authors have shown, authors can no longer be regarded as magisterial authorities (which is not to say that authors cannot have some authority); readers cannot be regarded as empty vessels into which author's messages are poured (which is not to say they will not go along with a story); and texts cannot be regarded as innocent representations of the world (which is not to say that they do not bear some relationships to the worlds they

49

describe and interpret). To some extent, Milorad Pavic's image of the author–text–reader relationship (two people holding a puma on ropes between them) suggests something of the dynamic tension of the relationship, but in the case of curricula, there are many 'authors', many 'texts' and many 'readers' in a complex web of relationships which defies the simplicity of the map metaphor, or even the simple puma and rope.

After considering the metaphors of maps and ropes, I outlined a general theoretical framework which might be useful for analysing some of the interdependencies which surround curricula, suggesting that they need to be thought of at least as a 'web'. But I also hastened to point out that this set of relationships (involving, for example, what might be called 'material practices' of communication, production-consumption and organisation) was no more than a collection of interpretive associations, no more than a table of invention for thinking about connections and contradictions in education and schooling. When we actually use such a framework, we quickly discover that the content and relationships it depicts are so diverse and complex that any simple idea of curriculum as 'text' dissolves. The relationships the table brings to mind will be various, depending on the readers' interpretations of every cell, let alone their interpretations of a curriculum or of the social world to be presented (can we any longer say 're-presented' with any certainty?) to a reader or user or student of a curriculum. Like Lawrence Durrell's story in *Justine* (the first of the 'Alexandria Quartet'), the story a curriculum tells is always a partial and incomplete understanding of what it hopes to describe.

Perhaps the most troublesome part of our traditional, 'modern' understanding of curriculum is the notion that there are straightforward, incontestable realities to which curriculum texts can correspond, and which curricula can represent. The tradition of correspondence and the assumption of representation are by now immensely powerful elements of our lived experience of curriculum (both our experiences as students and our experiences as teachers). We expect our curricula to 'point' unambiguously to features of the natural, material and social world. The notion of correspondence and the assumption of representation have been under attack in the philosophy of language and in the philosophy of science for much of this century, however. Few philosophers of language or science could now be found to defend these apparently 'commonsense' ideas. Instead, these philosophers are more likely to use images like that of the web to explain the relationships between the worlds of possibilities contained in language (think of Wittgenstein), the apparent coherence of the natural, physical and material worlds (think of Feyerabend or Toulmin), and the forms of social practice (including curriculum practice and textual practice) which hold our knowledge and action, our theories and practices, together in more or less coherent but always contested patterns (think of MacIntyre or Noddings or Benhabib). The experiments of contemporary novels simply dramatise these philosophical points—in their sometimes extravagant and fantastic ways, they communicate parallel insights: neither the text (and its relations to authors and readers), nor the world (and its relations to scientists and the users of science), nor the curriculum (and its relations to curriculum developers, teachers, students and communities) can be treated as an object with a nature and existence independent of the social and historical relationships which structure it for us. And perhaps the most liberating aspect of these insights is that coherence (truth?) is to be found in the activity of structuring the text, the world or the curriculum—activities which create specific sets of relationships between particular authors, texts and readers; between particular scientists, objects for study and users of scientific knowledge; or between specific curriculum makers, curricula and students.

In a postmodern world in which students are almost literally bombarded by information from strikingly diverse sources and in strikingly diverse media and forms, holding on to the old assumptions of correspondence and representation seems no more than a charming anachronism, a kind of whistling in the dark. There have never been, in all human history, such challenges to the magisterial authority of the teacher or the canonical authority of the text. The stories our curricula tell are heard, read and experienced amongst a cacophony of other stories. That is not to say that they are, or cannot be, more authoritative or instructive than other stories told in film, video-clips, newspapers or novels; it is just to assert that they are frequently pedantic and anachronistic survivors of an age where teachers and curricula were authoritative because they were rich sources of ideas and information in societies which were information-poor. Nor is it to say that curricula or teachers should emulate those other media and information sources; it is merely to say that they must acknowledge them and strive to pull together curriculum stories that can still educe understanding, skilled competence and social concern, and do so *despite* the contradictions and lacunae of the curriculum, teachers' and students' experience. Perhaps the contemporary novel offers models for those better stories—but perhaps to emulate them would also be to make concessions to the fantastic imagery and stunned passivity which characterise mass media and mass culture in the postmodern world. What these novels teach, I submit, is that textual practice is an active process of construction of relationships between authors, texts and readers, and that our task as curriculum makers and teachers is not only to tell curriculum stories to students but also to engage them actively in constructing stories for themselves, and in actively reconstructing the stories told by others. The point in this would not be just wordplay, experiments with imagery, or entertainment; nor is it to suggest that any story is as good as another. It is to suggest that the social practices of communication, production and social organisation impose their own imperatives which students can only come to understand through experience—through understanding how we are all affected by the consequences of miscommunication and misunderstanding, inadequate and exploitative forms of production and consumption, and misorganisation, disorganisation and injustice.

Of course, we have no alternative but to create and tell curriculum stories to our students, or to help teachers in constructing the work of teaching and learning in their classrooms. But we must be aware of the ambiguity of curriculum texts, and aware of at least some of their silences and lacunae. If schools and schooling are to proceed in anything like the way they do today, and have done for some centuries, we have no alternative but to do our best to create the webs of meaning and skills and social orientations which will allow students to see themselves in the wider web of our society. We would do well, however, to make them aware of the frailties of our stories and webs—in the same way that contemporary authors have done by unmasking the game of writing and reading novels. To understand—and to practise—the art and science of representation which underpins the development of curricula, we may need to remind ourselves and our students of the art of representation in science and the science of representation in art. When it comes to the difficult task of making curricula, it is not that we have no valuable knowledge to transmit, no valuable traditions of social practice to make available to students, no insights into social structuring (the structurings of culture, the economy and political life), or no insights into the limitedness and partiality of the social media which bind our individual identities in ideological frameworks shaped and constrained by the social media of language, work and power. On the contrary, we have much to tell about how we have been limited and constrained, as a society, through history and, as individuals, through our own biographies. We have no option but to tell these stories and to show how they have both empowered and disempowered people, and to show that possibilities for greater human emancipation through education are always before us.

The curriculum is a social medium, constructed and constrained as all media are. The world it 'represents' is manifold and diverse, always subject to interpretation, construction and reconstruction. We can no longer be naive about the possibility that a curriculum can provide a canonical text for students (like the divine inspiration of the carpet or the city in Calvino's image). There are just webs, and there is no alternative to having webs. It is disconcerting that there is no other possibility, but our knowledge that there is no other possibility may also encourage us to make better stories in curriculum, to be more respectful of the 'readers' of curriculum (students, parents and others) and more engaging in the ways we relate to them, more conscious about who the 'authors' of curricula are (both inside and outside education systems) and about the potential and limitations of their vision, and more conscious of the fragility of our texts —good stories, we hope, which will offer our students still greater opportunities to live meaningful, productive, satisfying and humane lives, in a complex world badly disfigured by irrationality, injustice and suffering. Knowing their frailty, we may still strive to create curricula which provide teachers and students with resources for building a better world from the imperfect and fragmentary materials we have bequeathed them.

Images from Morwell, Melbourne and the Moon: Curriculum as an element in the 'extended family of eyes'[1]

Lindsay Fitzclarence

Introduction

Guy Debord's book *The Society of the Spectacle* provides a powerful form of imagery for thinking about a culture. It begins: 'In societies where modern conditions of production prevail, all of life presents itself as an immense accumulation of *spectacles*. Everything that was directly lived has moved away into a representation' (Debord 1983, para. 1). Debord's assertion will be used as a way into the structure and argument of this chapter. His work contains the symbols which will be used to develop an account which attempts to hold together the ideas and practices associated with curriculum, technology and textual practice.

As a working proposition, I want to claim that we live in a society which is increasingly constructed around the imperatives of a dominant ideology. The ideology is one formed around the trading of *information*. The curriculum, technology and associated language we use to describe the way we live are aspects of this information form.

What we require is an analysis that is capable of holding these three elements together. Accordingly, I will develop this idea here by attempting to put the changes in curriculum, technology and language within a cultural context, a framework which recognises the significance of the founding practices, ideas and values which are shared by a group of people. Hence, curriculum and technology will be explored against a background of a sense of cultural changes and themes. The discussion will concentrate on the world of *image*, mainly because I find the critiques of what has been called the 'postmodern condition', with its stress on image, provide powerful metaphors to start to think about taken-for-granted things like the curriculum and television screens. At the same time, I want to think

---

1   I thank Jane Kenway and Bill Green for suggestions about the structure of the original presentation.

about changing patterns of human interchange, in order to throw some light on the formation of the person and the formation of society.

To begin with, however, there is a need for some working definitions, in order to help clarify the construction of some of the concepts that will frame this analysis.

information (noun)
—items of knowledge (*Australian Concise Oxford Dictionary* 1987, p.549)
—as (noun) communication of knowledge, transmission, dissemination, diffusion (*Roget's Thesaurus* 1966)

Information contains a number of associated words. These are:
inform (verb)—to impart a quality, to give shape to.
form (noun)—shape, arrangement of parts, visible aspect, shape of body.

When we look at the substructure of the word 'information', we find that, specifically in the words 'inform' and 'form', a material and concrete quality is being represented. We find a similar quality associated with the next term I want to consider here: 'image'.

The earliest definition of the word 'image' was 'a representation of a physical figure, or likeness'. The physical sense of the word was predominant until the seventeenth century; since that time, the word 'image' has been widely used as a mental concept, that is as simile or metaphor. Raymond Williams (1976) argues that 'image' is now used as a term in publicity ('perceived reputation'):

> This is in effect a jargon term of commercial advertising and public relations. Its relevance has been increased by the growing importance of visual media such as television. The sense of *image* in literature and painting has already been developed to describe the basic units of composition in film. This technical sense in practice supports the commercial and manipulative processes of *image* as 'perceived' reputation or character. (Williams 1976, pp.130–1)

The ubiquitous 'fax' is a good example of the shift in emphasis of the use of the word image, which Williams is describing. The word 'facsimile' is derived from the Latin *fac* as imperative of *facere*, 'to make', plus *simils*, 'like'. It gives us the noun 'facsimile' to denote an exact copy, especially of writing, printing, picture, system of producing this by radio transmission of signal from scanning (*Australian Concise Oxford Dictionary* 1987, p.370). What we find here is a fusion of the physical and mental connotations of the word. As noted in Williams's account, technology becomes a key feature in the development of the concept.

Curriculum, another of the terms in question here, is 'the development of that knowledge, thought and practice which is required by young people to enable them to take part in the production and reproduction of social life, and to come to know the character of these processes' (White 1985, p.78). This definition builds on the insights of radical education scholarship which notes that the curriculum can be really understood, *and* changed, only if it is seen in a social context.

To move on, let us begin with an 'image' of the curriculum. In the 1930s, the curriculum could be thought about in terms of formal specifications set down by a central authority (the Education Department) and controlled via standard documents (syllabi) and supervisors (district inspectors). The language of curriculum was relatively static, hierarchical and constructed outside the province of schools. Today, however, we can no longer think about the curriculum in these terms. We are now quite self-conscious about the political nature of the curriculum, the need to take account of the student, his or her 'agency', the multiple meanings carried by text, and the fact that schools and communities are dynamic sites of lived culture. We are accordingly provoked to think about curriculum in more elaborated ways than in the past. Notwithstanding this, I want to assert that we have not yet come to terms with the continuing impact of deep-seated logics which frame many of the changes unfolding in our lives, and which act to fuse curriculum, technology and language. Accordingly, we have not been very good at either interpreting the changes in the curriculum or constructing genuinely alternative practices. For example, accounts such as 'reproduction theory'—while offering significant insights about the class distortions produced and reproduced through the schooling process—have failed to help us make much sense of, and develop alternatives to, the dominant curriculum form. While the questions of social class distortion remain, and require an ongoing attempt to remediate and reform the structures which produce inequity, we also need strong accounts of the processes of social change. What we now require, that is, is a theory of culture which can position different aspects of social life as *interrelated*.

To return to the initial proposition, the analysis in this chapter will be developed around the idea that increasingly society in general and the person specifically are being constructed within a particular emphasis, one which is increasingly influenced by the communication, transmission, dissemination and diffusion of information. This emphasis is characterised in the person, as a specific unit of analysis, in terms of an excessive stress on the 'cognitive' aspects of reality, as an aspect of the world of information. For both society and person, such a tendency carries major contradictions. The constant stress on the construction of image and knowledge involves significant forms of imbalance and distortion. The constant stress on reconstruction and remaking, on change and innovation, is associated with destruction and instability. The biological/ecological stress we are now beginning to recognise as a global concern is associated with this trend.

What we urgently require, then, are genuine alternatives to the stress on 'information', and, relatedly, the stress on the 'cognitive'. Our definition of the healthy society and healthy person needs to be reworked.

Stories and images: beyond Morwell, Melbourne and the Moon

I want to consider these matters first by describing changes in the period since the Second World War via a highly personalised perspective. The reason for doing this will be become apparent as we proceed.

In 1956 I was seven years old and living in Morwell, a small country town in Victoria. Towards the end of that year, the Olympic Games were held in Melbourne, a city some ninety miles to the west of Morwell. At that time I had not been to Melbourne—in person, that is, or literally—but during the time of the Olympics I 'travelled' there via the medium of television. That television was introduced into Australia just prior to the Games probably needs to be pointed out.

I have vivid memories of one event from this time. One evening, I stood in a crowd of people who watched the final of the men's high jump on a television set in a shop window. In the failing light of the evening I stood amongst a large group of people who watched the gods Dumas and Porter struggle for the gold medal. I remember being enthralled by the image in the shop window, not just because of the sporting spectacle but also because of the magic of television. For the next couple of weeks, the children of my neighbourhood all played 'Olympics'.

Let us move on a few years. In 1963 I was thirteen and lived in the dualist world of many teenage boys. Life was divided equally: between summer and winter, football and cricket. In the summer of 1962/3, England and Australia were contesting an Ashes series. I was a keen witness of the cricket battles of that summer. By the Fourth Test, in Adelaide, the two teams had won a Test each, and the series was evenly balanced. Public interest was high, and moves were made to televise the Test. For two hours a day, during the tea-to-stumps period, a plane was flown around in a large circle over the border between South Australia and Victoria. Thanks to the signal relayed via this proto-satellite, we watched part of the Test each day. It was to be another ten years before I actually—that is, physically—visited Adelaide.

In 1969 I was a student at Melbourne University. In July of that year I took a day off classes and watched Neil Armstrong become the first person to walk on the moon. It was a momentous happening, probably because of the deeply entrenched mythology associated with the moon, but looking back on it I probably did not feel very much different from the way I felt that evening when I 'visited' Melbourne as a seven-year-old. The awe at technology opening up 'other worlds' was the common factor. The increasing significance of the world of *image* is, then, another key factor in this narrative.

Let us try to make sense of what is being discussed here. I am describing a process of 'displacement'. The term is meant to denote the process of 'shifting from its place ...' (*Australian Concise Oxford Dictionary* 1987, p.297). It is a process of being, abstractly, carried away, a process in which the imagination plays a crucial role. In that sense, it is largely a mental process in terms of which the concrete and immediate becomes fused with the abstract and distant. It is about social relations constructed at a distance and without direct human presence.[2] This trend applies as much to the curriculum as to other social categories and practices.

In order to develop a clearer image of the factors associated with the trend being described here, I want to look back to some earlier work. I have chosen Charles Baudelaire's 'The eyes of the poor', which was written in 1864 (Baudelaire 1970, pp.52–3).[3] Before examining this piece, it is relevant to reflect on the socio-economic context of Paris of the 1860s. At that time, the city was being 'reconstructed'. Baron Haussmann, the Prefect of Paris, had been directed to construct a number of boulevards through the city. Marshall Berman writes of this process in the following way:

> The boulevards were only one part of a comprehensive system of urban planning that included central markets, bridges, sewers, water supply, the Opéra and other cultural palaces, a great network of parks ... The new construction wrecked hundreds of buildings, displaced uncounted thousands of people, destroyed whole neighborhoods that had lived for centuries. But it opened up the whole of the city, for the first time in history, to all of its inhabitants. Now, at last, it was possible to move not only within neighborhoods, but through them. Now after centuries of life as a cluster of isolated cells, Paris was becoming a unified physical and human space (Berman 1983, pp.150–1)

In order to comprehend the social side of this process, let us now return to Baudelaire (1970). He presents an account of a pair of lovers sitting in a recently constructed cafe on one of the new boulevards. As they sit, they are watched by a poor family who have wandered into the neighbourhood. Baudelaire's words invoke the sense of social displacement; it is about people staring into, and out of, windows, and gleaning images of other worlds. It is also about the collision of different themes, discomfort and awe, about poverty and wealth. His work is also about the process of the fusion of discrete elements of the life world. In this case, it has a literal and concrete dimension to it. His descriptions are about life in a changing system, one where shops, arcades, parks and lighting were being constructed. It is an image of technology applied to the urban environment.

The social interactions described in Baudelaire's work are also, however, a forecast of things to come. In a very real sense, the process described by Baudelaire, of the fusion of discrete parts of the life world, has been advanced greatly by more recent technological developments. In fact, the very language of his account remains today to describe links in such things as electronic mail. We have 'highways', 'pathways', 'lines' and

---

2   For a detailed description of the process being described here, see Sharp (1985).
3   The idea of this analysis has been taken from Marshall Berman's *All That Is Solid Melts Into Air* (Berman 1983).

'stations' that carry the modern images. In the 'global village' of the modern period, satellites, computers and television screens, not to mention high speed planes and trains, link up previously separate and discrete parts of the world. I want to stress the situation as thematic, as a process, in which social meaning is made in expanding networks of interaction, in terms of which society is 'stretched'. The association might be thought about as an 'extended "family of eyes" ' (Berman 1983, p.153) The contact is at the visual and the cognitive level, one in which actual physical presence is not an automatic and essential quality of exchange. As the rate of social change has accelerated, and become 'white hot' (see Giddens 1984), social interaction has become increasingly 'imagined'. With the greater sophistication of technology, the process of 'displacement' has become more abstract and devoid of direct human presence. This trend has been sometimes described as the 'postmodern condition'. This is a term which is used to signify a change in the very basis of society; a change which incorporates a new form of relationship between the individual and the larger society.

Let me return to the present now and take up the account with another story of images in windows. Recently I spent a morning in Melbourne with my eleven-year-old daughter Emma. As we walked along, we came to a travel agency which had a poster of Beijing, China, on display in the window. Emma remarked how peaceful the scene looked and then said: 'But it's not like that now!' She proceeded to recount her understanding of the Tiananmen Square killing of students and citizens in early June 1989. When I asked her how she knew of this event, she talked about a television program called 'BTN' ('Behind the News'), which her class watches at school. Along with her classmates, she is regularly 'displaced' via the international telecommunications network. Schoolchildren like Emma are postmodern students, children of the information era. We gain an insight into the social construction of such people through the following comment about film audiences:

> Younger audiences are emerging who appreciate less predictable formats other than narrative film or linear documentaries. They're attuned to fragmented images, bizarre editing, ambiguity, experimental use of sound and music, abstract art. They enjoy the challenge of being jarred and jolted. (Colbert 1989, p.14)

Curriculum, technology and the postmodern student

At this point, I want to talk more directly about curriculum. We are beginning to recognise themes in the way that the curriculum is both conceptualised and actualised. The world of information exchange is finding expression in schools just as it does in other settings. For example, it has been suggested that on present trends the next decade might start to see the disappearance of the teacher as we currently understand that role. The computer terminal might well take the place of the teacher and, indeed, might perform the task more efficiently. A computer teacher, Paul Butler, has taken a different position and has argued that:

> The young people of the future will surely need to interact in all manner of ways with all manner of people, not merely with pre-digested text on a computer screen, but with developing skills to cope with the continuing explosion of information, to assist in their search for meaning ...
>
> Teachers will play the role they have always played, acting as intermediaries between the individual learners in a society and the knowledge and beliefs which that society deems valuable enough to be passed on to the young. What will be different will be the role of technology in supporting the pupil–teacher relationship. (Butler 1989, p.3)

The idea that is common to both these positions is the increasingly central place of digitalised or computerised 'information' as an aspect of curriculum. Another writer, Neil Hooley, has summarised the changing curriculum situation by saying '... all schools at all year levels are grappling with the impact of information technology on society and are responding with new approaches and new areas of the curriculum' (Hooley 1989, p.3).

The link between technology and curriculum is well expressed in an attempt to predict the form of schooling in the twenty-first century. Colin Goodwin makes the following observations:

> The use of highly sophisticated satellite and fibre-optic technology will have transformed modes of teaching and learning. State-of-the-art teleconferencing facilities, with high-definition two-way television, will be standard in schools. This equipment will be backed up by highly developed videotex and facsimile capacities that will provide desired information and hard copy almost instantaneously.
>
> The use of geostationary satellites will make educational material available from both national and international sources. Schools will have simple switch-on mechanisms that will make programs stored in Bombay, Boston or Brisbane accessible at any time to students in, say, Braybrook. (Goodwin 1989, p.30)

There is a need for the empirical work to explore the trends that are unfolding in schools and the changing nature of the relationship between teacher and pupil, and between school and society. I want to build on that idea by reflecting on changes in the curriculum of the School of Education here at Deakin University, which might help shape some initial questions.

Deakin University's School of Education inherited aspects of its program and many of its staff from the State College, Geelong. This institution was responsible for the initial training of primary school teachers. The program was very skills-based, but it contained many areas of current developments in educational theory as well. It was very much a curriculum of direct exchange, between students and staff and teachers in schools. The curriculum was also constructed around a social life involving sporting, as well as artistic and musical, events. Much of the curriculum involved 'doing things together'. Excursions, field trips, camping programs, sporting contests with other institutions, concerts, plays and pantomimes were all part of the curriculum of the program. This program was structured on a set of propositions which valued some form of combination—or perhaps better still, *integration*—of cognitive, emotional, social and practical development. It is appropriate, then, to reflect on the way that the undergraduate program has evolved since the establishment of Deakin University.

The dominant emphasis of Deakin University's teacher education program is cognitive, with a practical dimension via school experience rounds. The cultural activities which were carried over from the State College program have nearly all disappeared. The social aspects which helped give the State College program a life form beyond the ideas level have been allowed to atrophy. The architectural arrangements in the present School of Education reflect this issue and perpetuate the problem. We offer the students few places to meet, talk and work. The one tangible concession to student work space which has become a social environment by default is our Education Computing Laboratory. Our program is an 'ideas' curriculum; it is largely about image construction and maintenance. The diversity within it is largely ideological. Rolland Paulston (1976) helps make sense of this point when he talks about a division of ideological positions in the curriculum around equilibrium and conflict positions. Our program is basically 'one-dimensional', as the information society invariably is, with differentiation existing within the ideological divisions on this plane. Students are encouraged to take up different value positions in response to the question of what constitutes worthwhile knowledge; the diversity in the program is associated with the different positions they take up, while the commonality is that the curriculum is basically about 'information'.

I believe we can glean some sense of the contradictory and possibly even pathological nature of this arrangement when we look at the choices students make in their 'general studies' (an optional part of the degree program in which the School of Education has little influence). Many students choose 'movement studies', a fact that has caused a good deal of concern to some staff members over the years. They view movement studies as a somewhat 'weak' option compared with other courses on offer. Compared with the high-status knowledge required in some of the other courses, the human movement option is seen to represent poor value, intellectually and educationally. This seems to be an expression of the value positions associated with the old mental/manual dichotomy. Ways of knowing that contain the remnants of manual activity are seen to be of inferior status to purely intellectual subjects. The question here, however, is this: do the students choose this particular branch of study, in part, precisely because it offers a curriculum experience which acknowledges the physical and social in contrast to the essentially cognitive offerings elsewhere? That is, should we think about this pattern as a possible expression of a lived sense of cultural contradiction?

The story of the development of the curriculum of the School of Education at Deakin University is, in my opinion, part of the story of the emergence of the postmodern condition, with its emphasis on 'information exchange'. If this assertion seems to be something of an overstatement, let us again stop to ponder the impact of information exchange on the world of school-age children.

In a letter to the Editor of the *Age*, seven-year-old Daniel Arber wrote:

> Men have wrecked the world. We need to stop them. They will kill everything. We will die so please try to stop men chopping down trees. (Arber 1989, p.12)

The reactions to this letter were rather passionate, as perhaps one might have anticipated. They focused on how such a young child should come to hold such views, and the role schools might have played in the process. What we can reflect on, here, is the fact that the letter shows that young children are inducted into the wide circuit of information exchange. To engage in ideas of a planetary scale requires a projection well beyond the immediate and local. To do this, we have to cast our vision onto far horizons, and this increasingly happens via the images of the mass media. This example seems to be a case of the images of the information society filtering down to a child who has to struggle to accommodate the messages he is receiving, within his framework of understanding about being in the world. The world of information and image appears to be taking an increasingly significant place in the structure of the curriculum. If we take British education as anything of an indicator of trends, we can see the central role of 'information' in contemporary curriculum thinking. The design and technology curriculum is the fourth national curriculum to be drafted, behind English, mathematics and science ('Goals set for primary schools' 1989, p.2).

Conclusion: beyond the one-dimensional?

There are a number of different critiques which have helped us start to think about the postmodern condition. Accordingly, we are now in a position to begin to think about a cultural politics that struggles against the contradictions of the increasingly dominant mode of the information society. I am thinking here of contradictions associated with the dominance of culture over nature, of the abstract over the concrete, of the machine over the body, and of the individual over the group. Within education, the value positions associated with these different dualisms have produced a stratified and divided curriculum. Doug White expresses the issue in the following way:

61

The multi-national curriculum is the curriculum of disembodied universals, of mind as an information-processing machine, of concepts and skills without moral and social judgment but with enormous manipulative power, an education in which culture (in the sense of the lives and meanings of people) has no place. That curriculum proposed the elevation of abstract skills over particular content, of universal cognitive principles over the actual conditions of life. (White 1983, p.6)

An alternative cultural politics incorporates a rethinking and alternative practice of the relationship between these elements; such a politics involves rethinking the relations between the curriculum and technology.

Personal and social groupings are made, and develop, in terms of patterns of interchange. Relationships that are dominated by the cognitivised world of image produce a distorted outcome of both person and society. Exchange can operate at a number of related levels based on recognition of both commonality and difference. It seems quite reasonable to think of the person as developing with a sense of being— gendered, geographically placed, constituted as a biological creature—as well as with a cultural identity linked to others, across time and space. Paul James graphically expresses the issue at stake here when he argues:

If we are to have a future other than one of homogenous blandness we may have to choose to stop treating historically received cultural practices and sensibilities as part of a global supermarket. We may have to base our lives around an association to one place, still reaching out to the rest of the world, but struggling against the particular oppressions and inequities of that place for long enough to develop a binding relationship both to the locale itself and to the others who have chosen to stay with us. (James 1988, p.11)

Implicit in this comment is a view which holds together a number of binary opposites, such as private/public, biological/cultural, male/female, concrete/abstract, rational/irrational. The politics of such a view involves elements which are self-consciously at once conservative and radical. Such a view is *conservative* in the sense of recognising that there are many aspects of social life which we need to retain, and at the same time it is *radical* in recognising that we require the capacity to reflect on and change some things. A counter-curriculum trend, therefore, stands in opposition to the idea of life constructed on a single plane, and would therefore be one which engages the information mode at the same time as working hard to incorporate other elements of tangible forms of contact, including aesthetic and practical forms of activity. As we now come to recognise that the more esoteric elements of culture cannot operate without an awareness of the wider biosphere, so we should recognise that forms of interaction which involve practical and cooperative forms of exchange continue to be socially important. This means resisting the seduction of a curriculum which is structured principally around the information mode, and instead thinking about a curriculum form which has a cultural richness, in drawing on different forms of development and exchange. An alternative, postmodern, curriculum is therefore likely to be one where students can learn about practical skills, and communal and cooperative life, *as well as* the more sophisticated theoretical aspects of culture. Students would be involved in a range of activities in which skills are developed, and in which such a schema places the new technologies within a comprehensive framework. That is, students would learn to work with technology and at the same time learn to place it in historical and social context. What I have in mind here, in short, is a curriculum of the Head, the Hand and the Heart.

References

Arber, D. (1989), Letter to the Editor, *Age*, 27 June.

'Goals set for primary schools' (1989), *Age*, 17 July, Education Age Extra.

Australian Concise Oxford Dictionary (1987), Oxford University Press, Melbourne.

Baudelaire, C. (1970), *Paris Spleen*, trans L. Varèse, New Directions, New York.

Berman, M. (1983), *All That Is Solid Melts into Air: The Experience of Modernity*, Verso, London.

Butler, P. (1989), 'Teacher–student nexus still vital in high-tech age', *Age*, 17 July, Education Age Extra.

Colbert, M. (1989), 'Public taste is catching up with British avante-garde film-makers', *Age*, 21 July.

Debord, G. (1977), *The Society of the Spectacle*, Black & Red, Detroit.

Giddens, A. (1984), *The Constitution of Society: Outline of the Theory of Structuration*, University of California Press, Berkeley & Los Angeles.

Goodwin, C. (1989), 'Public/private split will become a thing of the past', *Age*, 14 March.

Hooley, N. (1989), 'Technology as a radical agent for expanded programs', *Age*, 17 July, Education Age Extra.

James, P. (1988), 'Emigration and a sense of place', *Arena*, no.85, pp.5–11.

Paulston, R.G. (1976), *Conflicting Theories of Social and Educational Change: A Typological Review*, University Center for International Studies, University of Pittsburgh, Pittsburgh.

Roget's Thesaurus (1966), Penguin, Harmondsworth, UK.

Sharp, G. (1985), 'Constitutive abstraction and social practice', *Arena*, no.70, pp.48–82.

White, D. (1983), 'After the divided curriculum', *The Victorian Teacher*, vol.2, no.1, pp.6–7.

White, D. (1985), 'Education: Controlling the participants', *Arena*, no.72, pp.63–79.

Williams, R. (1976), *Keywords: A Vocabulary of Culture and Society*, Fontana, Glasgow.

Part II

Part II

Teaching technology

Peter Medway

Introduction

My main purpose is to draw attention to the significance of a widespread current innovation in school curricula: the inclusion of technology as a 'core' element for all students in the compulsory stage of schooling. The content of technology education can take many conceivable forms (with, incidentally, different implications for language experience and the teaching of English). The emerging dominant model, soon to be given a statutory basis in England, has many strengths. As a selection from the range of phenomena comprising technology in the modern world, however, it has serious limitations. If schools were to address technology more inclusively and adequately than is being proposed, and in particular were to give full weight to the social embeddedness of technological practices, a very different curriculum—and with it a different language curriculum—would be the result.

Technology as design

There are moves in a number of countries to replace or supplement vocationally oriented school technical courses with compulsory technology studies, seen as an element of general education for all. The main reason is the perceived economic need for whole populations, rather than simply specialist cadres, who understand technology. There are many possible emphases within technology education. Distinctions are made, for instance, between the learning of technology to acquire capability, learning about technology to acquire awareness or understanding, and learning through or with the aid of technology. The general field of technology from which technology education derives its agendas is clearly very broad and includes, at the least, *devices*, which may be both outcomes of and means towards technological activity (and it is these which are most prominent in popular conceptions of 'technology'), *bodies of technical knowledge and expertise*, and *sociotechnical practices*. In the emerging technology curriculum, however, a particular set of emphases is coming to be adopted through a definition of technology as a purposeful process resulting in the production of artefacts, systems or environments. This particular formulation comes from the report of the working group commissioned to write the specifications for the subject technology within the national curriculum which is to be compulsory for all pupils in state schools in England and Wales between the ages of five and sixteen (Department of Education and Science and the Welsh Office 1989). Because they see technology primarily as process, the group make 'capability'—the ability to engage in technological practice—and not 'knowledge' the aim which is to be tested.

Two aspects of this approach are worth dwelling on. The first is that artefacts, systems and environments are seen very broadly, so that outcomes of technological activity would include not just coffee tables and hacksaws, or electronic burglar alarms and CD players, but a picnic for twenty people, a new track suit, a supermarket checkout system, a playground or a new variety of melon. In contrast with what 'technology' means in some other education systems, the term does not primarily refer to computers, nor will it in this paper. (In the national curriculum computers come under 'information technology', which is dealt with separately.)

The second aspect, which I intend to address at greater length, is the nature of the 'purposeful process' which technology is primarily seen as. In traditional craft lessons students working from a printed drawing would fabricate identical artefacts of wood or metal, an exercise purely in manual skill and accuracy. In more recent practice students have often been given, as before, the overall dimensions of, say, a metal hacksaw, together with specifications for its main parts, but have been required in addition to design certain parts, such as the grip and the spindles, for themselves. The continuing tendency to enhance this element has culminated in the placing of *design* at the heart of the technological process in the new national curriculum subject, which has actually been renamed design and technology, 'to be spoken in one breath'. The working group identify the components of 'design and technological capability' as ' Identifying needs and opportunities' for design and technological activities, 'Generating a design proposal', 'Planning and making' and 'Appraising'.

There is widespread relief that the working group have defined the subject in terms of processes with such broad educational value. We could have had students being tested in recalling stress formulae, assembling gear systems or fault-tracing in electronic circuits. There is a belief that the group have got it right in a number of ways. First, their proposals reflect an understanding of the following features of technological activity as revealed by research:

1   Technological expertise is not a matter mainly of the application of knowledge, though knowledge is important. In placing capability at the centre of their aims, the group make it clear that the teaching of scientific and technological knowledge will not on its own produce technologists, though this will be an important part of their training.

The role which knowledge plays in technological activity is a particular one, in that there is no specific body of 'technological knowledge'. Rather, the knowledge by means of which a technological problem may be solved can be drawn from any discipline and a mixture of disciplines, eclectically and opportunistically. Much knowledge is not intrinsically 'technological' but becomes so by virtue of being used for technology. Even in school technology, students sometimes reject the body of knowledge they have been taught as relevant to a specific area of problem solving in favour of quite different sources. For example, to give his students the opportunity to apply their knowledge of the measurement of resistance in materials, a teacher set them the task of designing a device to test the tenderness of peas being boiled ready for freezing but had to accept one student's solution based on measuring the chemical changes which occur in peas when cooked.

2   Another feature of the distinctive relationship between technological activity and the knowledge on which it draws is that that knowledge is typically inadequate or exists only in a form inappropriate to the context. Although the oil industry appears highly science-based, David Yeomans and I found in the UK lubricants plant of a multinational oil company that the knowledge does not exist for predicting the characteristics of the specialist greases which were blended there, even though the composition of the constituents was able to be analysed with great precision. Technology is not applied science.

3   Since knowledge cannot be simply 'applied' in order to generate solutions to technological problems, technological capability involves other elements which are as essential as knowledge. The important ones are quite different from the routine-following, algorithmic procedures suggested by the idea of 'applications', and in fact involve judgment, tacit knowledge and 'feel'. Grease-making, we were told, is actually more like cookery than science. J.M. Staudenmaier (1985) refers to 'the uniquely pragmatic character of technological cognition'.

4   The process is typically *social* not individualistic. The working group emphasise learning to collaborate in joint technological endeavour.

The group, then, have got it right about technology, at least in some respects. There is wide approval also for their overall curricular intent, which is to raise the status of the practical in relation to the academic. 'Rehabilitating the practical' (Layton 1984) involves giving dignity to practical activity and acknowledging making and doing, equally with academic activity, as a valid manifestation of intelligence, and derives support from the study of the complex and sophisticated cognitive processes of practitioners such as architects, surgeons, doctors—and, of course, teachers—who typically deal with ill-defined problems and draw on knowledge in complex ways in solving them (see, especially, Schön 1983).

In the new national curriculum in England and Wales, design and technology will be the only remaining subject in which students act on the world. Although circumscribed within the confines of a subject, through its interpretation of 'the practical' it enacts what is potentially a radically alternative pedagogy. The learning sought is less *discipline-driven*, following the sequential logic of a subject, than *situation-driven* through engagement with the problems and opportunities presented by specific contexts.

Design and the language of curriculum

A technology education based on design has points of bearing on the learning of language and literacy. The first concerns experience of language. Students working in practical situations, and especially in collaborative activity (organising, coordinating action, reaching agreement on design and on the division of tasks, persuading, reporting and so on), but also in obtaining help, information and materials, use a language directly associated with action, whereas in the English curriculum language has few direct consequences in the world of action, beyond occasioning evaluative or appreciative responses from the teacher and an audience. Since English largely neglects that considerable proportion of the world's language which seeks to make a difference to states of affairs, the chance for students to experience it elsewhere, in design and technological activity, is to be welcomed.

Secondly, design and writing have much in common. Both, for instance, are processes the occurrence of which is not confined to those times when their overt manifestations, such as drawing or writing on paper, are in evidence. What is encoded with pencil or typewriter or word processor is generated partly on the spot, at the 'point of utterance', and partly in earlier mental activities which the subject would probably characterise not as designing or writing but as 'just thinking'. (One of the students we studied thought of some of his best ideas when he woke up during the night.) Again, both designers and writers experience 'blocks', and are visited by solutions which arrive seemingly from nowhere, though sometimes aided by heuristic procedures. Finally, the recursive and iterative nature of the processes is strikingly similar.

A pursuit of the parallels might be quite fruitful, not least for students. Seeing writing as a form of design would interestingly enhance a rhetorical approach emphasising texts as contrivances to induce effects in others. Conversely, we might think of designers as writing the environment we live in. (And we recall, with a shudder, that poets were for Stalin the 'engineers of the human soul'!) New technologies are in any case confronting us with the connections, not least in enabling us to store and transport both writing and graphical designs, along with music, in identical form in the same medium of the floppy disk.

Thirdly, we might note that neither 'technology' nor 'literature' can be identified by clear criteria and that both terms are used selectively as honorifics. Hence, what women do at home is less likely to be dignified with the label 'technology' than what men do at work.

My last point arises from the consideration that English has a repertoire of topics by talking and writing about which students are believed to develop their linguistic capabilities. The repertoire might be expanded beyond the biographical universals such as birth, death, love and accidents, the detail of personal experience in the private domain and a handful of ready-defined public 'issues', to take in (and dignify through attention) the working lives of people as maintainers, manipulators and modifiers of the material and technological base of the society. One could imagine an English program in which students interviewed engineers, food chemists, printers, cooks, medical technologists, clothes designers, traffic engineers and sound recording technicians, and collected the culture's narratives of invention, construction, problem solving, inspired adaptation and ingenious improvisation.

Technology as more than design

Design, however, does not exhaust technological activity, and in fact accounts for quite a small part of it. Much technological activity is getting things to work. Word processing, for example, is not normally seen as a technological activity, and indeed it is not when it consists simply of typing in text (even though schools may teach this in courses called 'information technology'). But as soon as you go beyond the basic procedures which the program offers you in a user-friendly way, and into areas where you have to make your own ways through (such as, in my experience, writing a macro which will extract an address from an address file, put it top left after the date in a letter and then, later, onto an envelope), then you are engaging in technological activity, one characterisation of which might be 'making things do things for you'.

Other technological activities are the maintenance of machines and systems, their repair, involving fault diagnosis, and their modification and customisation. Michael Scriven argues that even in the development of new machines, innumerable small modifications made by operatives may be as important as the conception of the original named designer. The steam engine as it first appeared was of little practical use: what made it step by step into an efficient machine offering worthwhile gains in productivity was 'the inspired tinkering of anonymous mine foremen': 'technologists are improvers, practical creators, fiddlers, perfectionists, analysts—and all those things can be found on the production line' (Scriven 1987).

Consider one student's experience of technological activity in the context of an assessed project, extending over many months, to develop a new device. Andrew, aged fifteen, had chosen to produce a radio-controlled shutter release for his camera, for use in wildlife photography.[1] At one point Andrew was considering using a solenoid motor to provide the force which would activate the shutter release directly on the receipt of a radio signal. (A solenoid is a motor which produces not a rotary motion but a single thrust in one direction: the solid core in the middle of the coil shoots out when current is applied to the coil.)

This is how Andrew explained to us the stage he had reached in developing his idea. As he spoke, he pointed to features on sketches and a mock-up device:

But I'm not going to use that idea now, or that one, I'm going to use some type of potential energy, like just using the solenoid to trigger something else off, because we can't find no solenoids. We're not really experienced enough to make one, to get one just right ... So, me and my uncle who's helping me a bit, we're going to work out something in the Christmas holidays that's using potential energy. Because he was quite a good engineer.

[How does that work, Andrew? I don't know what potential energy *is*.]

Where, like a mousetrap, where the mouse only has to touch the cheese very lightly and then it comes down to chop its head off ... so just using a little bit of energy to trigger off the lock. With a relay you can use just a little bit of power to let through a big 240 volts or something ...

... I went down to my uncle's one weekend and we didn't have any solenoids and stuff and so we had a look at what we'd got and we'd got some motors and things, so we thought we'd better do something that day, so we just made this up [indicating a device] which is made up with what we'd got. We'd just got a pinion [?] on the motor which drives onto this which has got a rubber grommet for a pulley, which is coming round here with an elastic band, then we grooved that out on an electric drill and put a bush in it, then this has got this cam on it which pushes that up like that ... so with this, when we use this on the camera, see, the camera release is mounted there and that held it secure with a washer in there. And so on this it was actually the rubber band that was firing the camera, and not the pressure from the motor.

[The reason you had to go for this spring mechanism is simply because you can't get the appropriate solenoid. That's amazing that you can't, actually. Is it possible to make a solenoid?]

Yes, it is possible to make them, but there's a lot of things to consider, like each turn of the wire has to be touching the one next to it and

---

1   It is, of course, significant that Andrew is a boy. In the research during which we met Andrew, Dave Yeomans and I found very few girls on elective technology courses. The issue of technology as a masculine practice is a huge one which I cannot begin to broach in this chapter. The research is reported in Medway and Yeomans (1988).

then you've got to take into consideration the thickness of the wire, how many turns you've got, how long each turn is, how long the barrel of the solenoid is, all different things and you have to read books and books about them before you can even start making them. Because me and my uncle did try making some ... We set a drill up with a screwdriver thing on it which gears it down so the drill goes round slower, then we put it in a vice so it was going slow, then we put a shaft on it and then we held a pen barrel in the chuck of the drill as well and then we put a cork on it and then cut it in half and spaced it and then we had it turning, with the wire feeding on the floor to make a solenoid, but ... and then we tried them, but they soon get too hot if you don't know what you're doing. Because we couldn't do one that didn't get hot. Mind you, we were using them on car batteries.

What this exemplifies is technological work as *situated cognition*, conducted not in abstraction at a drawing board but within a highly specific material and social context which provides agendas, resources, cues and clues, and constraints. (Typical of real technological work are such considerations as 'we thought we'd better do something that day'.) Adapting a point by John Seely Brown, Allan Collins and Paul Duguid (1989, p.32), what is going on here is not a deployment of knowledge within a situation which is essentially separable or neutral or can be seen as just 'context', but an engagement with knowledge in a way that is shaped by the situation: 'situations might be said to co-produce knowledge through activity'.[2] Andrew's situation-embedded mode of operating is typical of much technological activity outside design departments and is not adequately encompassed by the characterisation of technology as essentially design, with the implications that carries of a rationalistic goal-seeking trajectory followed in detachment from contextual mess. The 'mess' in which the technologist works is not only that of the original ill-defined situation but may also be that of the production environment, with its finite material resources and specific social relations.

The important underlying question is whether privileging design over other aspects of technological activity negates the intention to rehabilitate the practical, and denies recognition to those who innovate in more immediate, improvisatory and responsive ways and who 'think with their hands'. It tends to reduce the latter to the status of paratechnologists who are seen, like paramedics, as performing only the more routine procedures of the discipline without calling on intelligent creativity or deep knowledge. Might it be that, as Bill Green has speculated in conversation, behind the conception of the designer there lurks the image of the romantic poet, in contrast with whom the opportunistic *bricoleurs* and potterers, acting from shared social knowledge, appear as cloddish and dull? In the nineteenth century science education moved from a 'science of common things'—practical, related to agricultural and other trades, locally specific—to an abstract mental discipline functioning as a means of exclusion (Layton 1973). Is there perhaps a similar anti-democratic risk

---

2   Chris Bigum drew my attention to this paper.

that technology might be defined according to an idealistic conception of design identified with a small specialist elite who do not get their hands dirty?

Technology as social practice

My criticism of the design emphasis in technology education has been in terms of its lack of fit with the majority of technological practice. Referring again to the reality of technology in the contemporary world, I now want to indicate phenomena which suggest an educational agenda of a different kind. These phenomena are the changes which information technology facilitates in production and organisation and in the nature of work, including technological work. Here I rely entirely on the accounts of other researchers, and in particular those of Larry Hirschhorn (1984), Tessa Morris-Suzuki (1988), David Lyon (1988) and Robin Murray (1988).

The first phase of mechanisation produced machines which would do the same job endlessly. Those in Henry Ford's Model T Factory could each do one job only. Adjusting the machines for a new process was a long and costly business: hence the importance in the Fordist factory of long runs of standardised products for a market which presented, or had to be persuaded to present, a uniform demand. A lot of expensive design went into the product and had to last a long time; but as the production run went on into thousands and millions of units, the proportion of design cost to materials cost fell and fell. In contemporary jargon, the information content declined in relation to the materials content. Redesigning and re-tooling for a new product were forbiddingly expensive; the River Rouge plant was closed for nine months when production switched from the Model T. When the new run was shortlived, as with the Ford Edsel, the costs were immense. Innovation was thus a desperate last resort when all else had failed. The machines were rigid and inflexible because what they were to do was built into the very structure of cogs and cams which determined the direction and speed of movement.

In more recent machines, however, the parts may be individually controlled by separate power sources—electrical, hydraulic, pneumatic or whatever—which can be independently varied. 'What the machine does', therefore, is determined only within limits by its structure. The detail of its operation is determined by controlling the power sources, which may in turn be controlled by a computer program. Thus the information formerly built into the structure is now held separately from the machine, in easily modified computer software. General Motors, with the most up-to-date versions of the pre-computer machine tools, could, we are told, reset a body pressing machine in eight hours. Nissan and Toyota, with CNC (computer numerically controlled) machines, take one and a half minutes.

The post-Fordist factory (of which the best examples are not in car manufacturing but in other sectors, including clothing) is therefore able to switch production rapidly and without the necessity to follow up with a long run. Diversity of product lines and small-batch production become possible. These also become necessary as the individualisation of needs and tastes, and the generating of new ones, are promoted in the consumer not only by advertising but by developments in the culture as a whole (including, incidentally, English teaching, which from the 1960s encouraged students to identify, reflect on, and amplify whatever was unique and different in their personalities and 'needs'.) Rapid change is the order of the day: four fashions each season instead of the former one. Firms keep ahead by constant innovation.

Technology, particularly information technology, both enables firms to innovate and helps them decide in what direction to innovate. The Italian clothing firm Benetton is linked by computer to its thousands of outlets so that trends in sales may be instantly translated into production specifications; goods are produced 'just in time' by hundreds of sub-contracted small firms, and no money is tied up in stocks.

The firms which survive produce organisational structures and cultures to maximise the possibilities of fruitful innovation and rapid adaptive response. Their features are flattened hierarchies, lateral rather than vertical communications, networks rather than fixed structures, and the instilling of a few simple corporate aims and ethics rather than long job descriptions and tight discipline. Ideas are sought from everyone, irrespective of their status in the organisation. The post-Fordist firm learns from community groups, the Greens, and small cooperatives and guerrilla groups, and cares for its people more carefully than for its machines. Seek out 'the gold in the workers' heads' is the Japanese slogan.

Product development comes not only from the protracted design process of a separate 'R and D' team, but also from constant small changes in the course of production: Scriven's inspired tinkerers have full scope again in the adaptable machines of the computer age. And whereas a snarl-up in the Ford factory was a disaster by causing costly delay, Japanese post-Fordist culture welcomes perturbations in the system as making possible the learning which will produce the next advance and a new competitive edge. The firm has become a *learning organisation*.

The emergence of the post-Fordist model is certainly uneven (food retailing is just, with Macdonalds, entering the Fordist stage), and there is no reason to believe that it will determine the shape of most work in the future. The account which I have just given is, moreover, undoubtedly an idealisation; the post-Fordist firm may simply have found new ways of exploiting its workers (see, for instance, Watkins 1989). But whereas the phenomenon is not necessarily a cause for celebration, it undoubtedly needs to be noted for the different opportunities and constraints it offers for people's working lives. Not the least of its significance is the suggestions it evokes by analogy for developments in sectors other than production, including education. It invites speculation, for instance, about the characteristics of a post-Fordist school and curriculum which, instead of depending on standardisation, fixed groupings and timetables, inflexible plant, rules and tests, prespecified knowledge, departments and hierarchies, would be responsive to individual needs, would shift groupings of both students and teachers opportunistically, would blur the distinctions between teachers and students and between both and others outside, would bring knowledge to bear at point of need in the context of specific tasks, and would blur the distinction between productive work and learning. Learning styles like Andrew's would be *with*, not *against*, the grain of such a school.

There is more to be said about the worker and technology in the latest manifestations of the factory. Note that what we had in my description was not the dream of automation: the workers are still there. The dream has, in fact, never been realised, although it goes back a long way. Mechanisation aimed at machines which would work together without human intervention by natural laws, like the solar system; but machines go out of adjustment through wear and through changes in vibration, heat and so on, so that constant supervision and adjustment are needed.

Cybernation appeared to hold out the promise of a solution: the so-called 'error' from varying conditions was imported into the feedback loop and activated continually compensating movements. But removal of the workers again proved unattainable and is likely to remain so: the complexity of the systems led to new sources of error and unanticipated interactions. Misplaced trust in the autonomy of the system leads to Three Mile Island—and to a possible nuclear exchange.

What we have now, therefore, is an acceptance that human agency is here to stay in the factory and a new attempt to maximise the effectiveness of the contributions which only people can make. According to Hirschhorn (1984, p.2), the 'postindustrial conception of work and technology' is that the machine is constantly developed by the workers, through adjustments to the software, in response to mishaps. As the workers learn, they incorporate their learning into the system. At the same time information technology provides the workers with the data, from sensors and from stored traces of past activity, to maximise their chances of pattern-spotting and of developing an intuitive *Gestalt* feel for the whole of a complex system, just as the craft worker had a feel for the individual small machine. If the factory is a 'text', the worker is helped by the computer to 'read' it, and then to 'write' it. Thus 'the post-industrial machine evolves' as the worker learns. Hirschhorn claimed in 1980 that in the US there were five hundred so-called 'sociotechnical' factories which ran on these lines, placing a premium on the capacity of the workers to develop the machine. He speculates that such regimes 'may help to bring out in the culture a developmental concept of the self, a concept that leads people to seek out learning opportunities throughout their lives' (Hirschhorn 1984, p.4).

Again, we can envisage parallel developments in schools, resulting perhaps in a curriculum which becomes progressively less opaque and arbitrary-seeming to the students as they are helped by supportive information systems to understand it as a whole, to find individual routes through it, and finally to customise it for themselves and have their customisations incorporated as resources available to all.

Rather than 'design capability', the essential core of the technology curriculum might be critical awareness of the role which technology is playing in changes in the economy and society—with emphasis on the critical. What tends to be promoted in and out of school is adulatory, asocial and apolitical hype about the coming 'information society'. The claims are about democratisation through universal online access to data and even to decision making, decentralisation (go to the office via the modem while remaining in the bosom of your family in a rural retreat), and dispersal of power. The reality is that information technology is developed and promoted more for military purposes than any other, that databanks are controlled by the entrepreneurs and corporations who own the media, that information technology enhances the power of the powerful to control and to exercise surveillance, that ethnic, class and gender differences, and on a global scale, North/South differences, are reinforced, and that the 'electronic cottage' conceals the desperation, tedium and discomfort of visual display unit piecework compounded by the proximity of squalling kids (cf. Lyon 1988).

What above all needs to be resisted is *technological determinism*, the belief that technology is an inexorable force in its own right, that its advance can only be accepted, and that questioning it is Luddism. It is a matter not of simply resisting but of understanding that technology is socially shaped and contestable: information technology clearly has the potential to enhance either democracy or subjugation.

The critical tradition within the subject might make English teachers particularly effective promoters of the enquiry and appraisal which students need to undertake in relation to technology. The biographies and case studies which students construct as part of their English work might include tales of self-fulfilment through technological activity and production but also those of marginalisation and alienation: people displaced from jobs by new machines, for instance, and the computer junkies and hackers for whom machines are a preferable alternative to people. English itself should use technology, and especially the word processor, but in this, too, should promote the critical attitude which is a vital part of technological education. How often, for instance, are students invited, after their introduction to word processing, to evaluate what it adds to and takes away from their capability as writers? And if a pair of jeans, a six-pack and other technological products are texts, should we not be helping students to read them in the way that we help them read media?

Technology and textual practice in school
My final section can be no more than a brief note. Technology and textual practice come together in school in three ways. First, as I have suggested, students talk, read and write in the pursuit of technological activities. Any technological activity beyond the simplest depends heavily on language, a language very different from that which is practised and studied in English. Secondly, students ought, as part of their technological education, to generate texts about technology. They might do this in English, as well as elsewhere. Thirdly, a point I have hardly touched on and have space only to mention, computer-based technology is now

77

transforming textual practice itself. Word processing, for instance, goes far beyond computerised typewriting and enables the rapid merging of multiple texts and machine-driven modifications of style. New forms of text are possible, structured in layers or networks (hypertext) rather than sequentially. The dissemination of text online or on disks makes problematic the notion of publishing and enables 'readers' to make their own modification of texts. Computer-generated text and computer translation raise questions about the association of language with human intention.[3] To offer students the experience of these new processes and, more importantly, the chance to reflect critically on their implications might well be seen as a central part both of technology education and of language education.

References

Brown, J.S., Collins, A. & Duguid, P. (1989), 'Situated cognition and the culture of learning', *Educational Researcher*, vol.18, no.1, pp.32–42.

Department of Education and Science and the Welsh Office (1989), *Design and Technology for Ages 5 to 16: Proposals of the Secretary of State for Education and Science and the Secretary of State for Wales*, HMSO, London.

Hirschhorn, L. (1984), *Beyond Mechanization: Work and Technology in a Postindustrial Age*, Massachusetts Institute of Technology Press, Cambridge, Mass.

Lanham, R.A. (1989), 'The electronic word: Literary study and the digital revolution', *New Literary History*, vol.20, no.2, pp.265–90.

Layton, D. (1973), *Science for the People*, Allen & Unwin, London.

Layton, D. (ed.) (1984), *The Alternative Road: The Rehabilitation of the Practical*, Centre for Studies in Science and Mathematics Education, University of Leeds, Leeds, UK.

Lyon, D. (1988), *The Information Society: Issues and Illusions*, Polity Press, Cambridge.

Medway, P. & Yeomans, D. (1988), *Technology Projects in the Fifth Year*, Manpower Services Commission, London.

Morris-Suzuki, T. (1988), *Beyond Computopia*, Kegan Paul International, London.

Murray, R. (1988), 'Life after Henry (Ford)', *Marxism Today*, October, pp.8–13.

Schön, D. (1983), *The Reflective Practitioner: How Professionals Think in Action*, Basic Books, New York.

Scriven, M. (1987), The rights of technology in education: The need for consciousness-raising, Paper commissioned by the Minister for Education and Technology in South Australia, University of Western Australia, Perth.

---

3 There is a stimulating discussion of these issues by Richard Lanham (1989) in his article 'The electronic word: Literary study and the digital revolution'.

Staudenmaier, J.M. (1985), *Technology's Storytellers: Reweaving the Human Fabric*, Society for the History of Technology and Massachusetts Institute of Technology Press, Cambridge, Mass.

Watkins, P. (1989), 'Flexible manufacturing, flexible technology and flexible education: Visions of the post-Fordist economic solution', in J. Sachs, N. Russell & G. Chataway, *Technology and Education; Forging Links with Business and Industry*, Gold Coast College of Advanced Education, Surfers Paradise, Qld.

Curriculum and the new mythinformation technologies[1]

Chris Bigum

Coming to terms with the new information technologies in schools

Computers and their high-technology relatives have been widely used in schools since the early 1980s. Since then there has been a steady growth in the numbers of computers and a shift to newer models as schools battle with the exhortations to participate in the so-called information age. It is fair to say that during this time the prime concern of schools and school systems has been to come to terms with computers, to be seen to be doing something, almost anything, as long as computers were involved.

Schools, however, will more than likely suggest that they have developed a curriculum response to the changes that have occurred in the world outside school. I want to argue that the response has been to a narrow, technicist description of the world, largely constructed by vendors of high-technology products and romantically portrayed by an uncritical media. In responding, schools have actually coupled the way they talk about computers and schooling to the way that vendors and other public discourses talk about computers and education. This response, as this chapter will argue, both implicates schools in the construction of a particular public discourse of the new information technologies and inhibits in schools the development of curricula that are able to question adequately many of the claims made on behalf of the new information technologies generally and in schools in particular.

Most accounts of technologies and curriculum have been developed within discourses similar to those which have positioned computers in schools. In most accounts, assumptions about the nature of technology and of curriculum are made which make it difficult to 'read' what is going on in a wider social and cultural frame. This chapter examines a small selection of the work of scholars who have to some degree focused on curriculum and the new information technologies. This selection indicates some of the different discursive framings that have been developed as a

---

1   The term 'mythinformation technologies' was coined by Langdon Winner (1989).

consequence of using computers and their related technologies in schools. The accounts are necessarily brief and are intended to indicate the theoretical framing that is employed in each analysis.

Cuban: teachers and machines

Larry Cuban published his book on the classroom use of technology since 1920, in 1986. He conducted a study of the history of television use in schools, and then, as a result of his findings, decided to extend the study to include film and radio. At the time of this research computers were being heralded in schools as a significant 'new machine', and so he extended his study to include computers as well. The opening paragraph of his Introduction captures something of his thinking about machines in classrooms:

> Some images stick in the mind like a thistle to a pant leg. A few years ago, while researching how teachers taught in the 1920s, I came across a 1927 National Archives photograph of a Los Angeles teacher in the midst of a geography lesson in the cabin of an airplane [see accompanying photograph]. Here was an aerial classroom of students viewing urban geography firsthand; this was to demonstrate clearly how progressive education had influenced the city's teacher corps. In the photo, the teacher, standing in the front of the cabin near a small chalkboard, pointed to a globe as she talked to seven children sitting two abreast in desks facing her. The juxtaposition of an aerial classroom, the apex of modern technology in 1927, with a teacher, instructing the class in a totally earthbound, familiar manner, seemed to be a symbolic shorthand for the perennial paradox facing public schools: constancy amid change. (Cuban 1986, p.1)

The parallels between this image and contemporary media representations of the new information technologies in today's classrooms are strong. Out-of-the-ordinary accounts of computers in classrooms are almost the norm in media accounts of the new information technologies in schools. If Cuban's account of the 'mile high' geography lesson is indicative of media accounts of high-tech schooling in the 1920s, then the media's propensity for reporting the unusual and the spectacular in education has a long history. While reporting 'sea level' geography classes may be less appealing to the media, the valorising of such practices makes a significant contribution to a public discourse of curriculum and technology. There is, of course, more than one way to 'read' the photograph. The depiction showing teachers and classrooms going about their usual work reaffirms that things have not changed much in schools during this century. The association of the 'new' technology of flying machines with education is also important in attributing higher purpose to the technology than mere transport. Cuban's 'reading' identifies an idea that runs through his book: the paradox of constancy in change.

With the benefit of hindsight, Cuban's recounting of the history of film, radio and television makes fascinating reading for those interested in the new information technologies in the classroom. The obligatory, enthusiastic claims made on behalf of each technology at the beginning of its introduction into classrooms is not at all difficult to map onto the claims made on behalf of computers. Not only were there claims about revolution and replacement of textbooks, but a discourse that reconstructed teachers' roles in terms of *managers* of the new machines was also evident.

Cuban adopts a position which seeks to interpret from the teacher's perspective what has happened with a range of information technologies. He documents the arguments that blame teachers for the poor acceptance of electronic technologies in the classroom. Teachers who feel guilty or uncomfortable about not embracing computer technology in their teaching today may take reassurance from the fact that, since the 1920s at least, many teachers have adopted similar positions about 'new' information technology in their classrooms. Cuban's striking finding is that, at least in America, teachers found only a very small classroom role for media like radio, television and film. Putting arguments about teacher hostility towards electronic technologies in the classroom in perspective, he points to the significant changes in teaching practice that have occurred and argues that:

> The changes teachers have embraced, however, have solved problems that teachers identified as important, not necessarily ones defined by nonteachers. Moreover, what teachers adopted buttressed their authority, rather than undermining it. Thus, those technologies incorporated into routine teacher practice responded to daily classroom needs without undercutting the teacher's control of the class. (Cuban 1986, pp.65–6)

In the end Cuban comes down to what he terms 'situationally constrained choice' as the basis for change. The teacher is portrayed as the gatekeeper of the classroom, keeping out all but a little of the information technologies that Cuban studied.

Cuban's account of computers in American schools (Cuban 1986, pp. 72–103) is useful reading. He successfully maps the early trends of using computers in classrooms onto his earlier accounts of film, television and radio. He accurately depicts the confusion and the 'intense internal uncertainty' that exists over how to make best use of this technology, and in the end he comes down strongly in favour of hastening slowly, arguing that there are other notable instances of applying technical solutions to social problems with disastrous results.

Cuban's work is important. It locates each new technology as an innovation in educational technology, as a new technology amid other classroom technologies. It portrays the teacher as the master engineer, the one who chooses and controls whatever technologies are used in the classroom within the constraints of schooling. In this sense it is a study located in the culture of the classroom, one which accepts the technology as a given and is only mildly curious about discourses which take technologies built for other social purposes and locate them in classrooms.

At the end of his book Cuban offers a useful critique of those who locate machines in classrooms in terms of planned change. Had he written his book a few years later, he would have found Lucy Suchman's (1987) excellent account of plans and situated actions germane to his analysis. Framing studies of machines in classrooms in terms of change, he argues that most research fails to take a sufficiently long look, and that when a longer perspective is taken change is clearly identifiable, but little of what is identified as change was intended or planned externally.

Schostak: breaking into the curriculum
A book edited by John Schostak and published in 1988 draws upon the work of the 'Teaching, Handling Information and Learning' project undertaken by the Centre for Applied Research in Education (CARE) in the School of Education at the University of East Anglia. In his opening contribution to the collection, Schostak (1988a) adopts a broad, eclectic perspective of curriculum. His theme of 'breaking into the curriculum' is derived from the practice known in computing circles as 'hacking'. In its pejorative sense hacking means 'illegally breaking into computers or software.[2] The term is also applied to a 'quick and dirty' style of computer programming; that is, one hacks a piece of code. Schostak employs the term in a more romantic sense, arguing that 'breaking in' or 'hacking into' school structures is a necessary part of education:

---

2   Now that software manufacturers no longer copy-protect their products, this is a less common practice.

84

Breaking into the curriculum has to do with revealing and challenging these structures in ways which give children access to the knowledge and power to influence their own lives. (Schostak 1988a, p.5)

In elaborating his argument about information technology and curriculum in another article in the book, the other metaphor Schostak (1988b) relies upon is the *game*. He argues that games and schooling (which he describes as a kind of game) are as much about the construction and manipulation of ignorance as they are about knowledge.[3] He makes a bald distinction between schooling (bad) and education (good) and argues that the kind of flexibility of problem-solving approaches supported in adventure games is an important educational model. It is a romantic, liberal view of education and curriculum and a correspondingly romantic, liberal view of the new information technologies. It has some of the overtones of Seymour Papert's early musings about the impact of computers in schools.[4]

Schostak's understandings of what a computer can contribute to educational process do not suffer from the critical concerns of Chet Bowers (1988), who asks important questions about, among other things, the kinds of information that will be stored on computer and the kinds of information and representations that will not. Nor do they suffer from the kinds of criticisms that writers like Langdon Winner (1989) and Jean-Pierre Dupuy (1980) make of the new information technologies; for instance, that they confuse an enormous supply of information with the wisdom to make use of it, or assume that the communicative potential of the kinds of computers to be found in schools can somehow compete with the computer and communications power available to large corporations and government bureaucracies.

While Schostak extends his account of information technology and curriculum to wider social issues, his purpose is to celebrate the possibilities rather than to ask the kinds of questions of technology that he asks of schooling. In articulating his major criticism of schooling, he offers us a useful question to ask about the development and use of the new information technologies:

The curriculum form of current schooling is thus largely political and ineducative since children have virtually no access to the educational processes which open up the hidden structures, the ulterior motives which form the underlying gameplan of schooling. (Schostak 1988b, p.112)

---

3   If the world and schooling can be reduced to a set of games, then we must ask the game identifiers what game they are playing and what are their rules.
4   Papert has spoken about the computer as Trojan horse, a metaphor not unlike that proposed here for breaking into the Trojan city of schooling. Of course, there are few who, like the Cassandra of Greek mythology, warn us to be wary of today's 'high-technology' Greeks bearing gifts!

A simple substitution of 'new information technologies' or 'computing' for 'schooling' will produce the question that is rarely asked about computers and curriculum or the new information technologies and society.

Schostak's book is also important because it represents a discourse that would identify some of its intellectual base in the critical educational literature[5] and uses the new information technologies as a kind of new tool with which to revitalise the work of critical pedagogy. In a sense it is a marker for many teachers who can exercise sound criticism of certain practices of schooling but seem hypnotised by the claims made on behalf of the new information technologies in education.

Hamilton: axe heads and other educational tools

In his little blue book about curriculum, David Hamilton (1987) offers some useful ideas about what he terms 'the complex relationship between tools and pedagogy'. Leaving aside the problems in using a word like 'tool' which currently carries meanings of neutrality in expressions like 'a computer is just a tool', Hamilton offers a historical perspective that usefully includes many of the social technologies of schooling. If we are sceptical about the millennial claims made on behalf of the new information technologies by others, Hamilton's analysis is useful in that he shows that computers can be understood, in curriculum terms, like other educational technologies.

Importantly, Hamilton defines a resource or technology as educational if it facilitates an educational goal. This definition contrasts with the definition of material educational technologies that acquire their educational attributes from the claims of vendors. For Hamilton, acquiring an educational epithet is only an indication of more significant curriculum change. He argues that:

> ... when teachers change from textbooks to worksheets; or learners change from slide-rules to electronic calculators the pedagogy changes and a different range of experiences and options are made available. (Hamilton 1987, p.61)

This comment contrasts with the typical questions which seek to compare (somehow) the pedagogy employing one technology with the pedagogy employing another. That such questions have been important in shaping the pedagogical discourse concerning computers in classrooms is indicated by an early paper by Seymour Papert (1972). In it Papert parodied the application of the scientific model to the evaluation of computer-based learning. He suggested that the failure to find significant differences in favour of computer-based approaches was like the failure of a

---

5   Freire, Shor, Stenhouse, Kohl and Stuart are mentioned in one of Schostak's papers (1988c, p.158)

nineteenth-century engineer who tried to show that engines were better than horses:

> This he did by hitching a 1/8 HP motor in parallel with his team of four strong stallions. After a year of statistical research he announced a significant difference. However, it was generally thought that there was a Hawthorne effect on the horses ... the purring of the motor made them pull harder. (Papert 1972, p.2)

Hamilton makes a number of points that can be usefully applied to thinking about the new information technologies and curriculum:

- From his research on the history of schooling, Hamilton points to the often asynchronous relationship between technology and pedagogical change. He argues that sometimes a particular technology had to wait until educational ideas emerged that could make use of the technology.

  As schools become increasingly reconstructed as important market sites,[6] it is likely that any possible asynchrony between technology and pedagogical change will be lost as each new range of high-tech consumer products is defined as significant/essential for schools. The improved articulation between computer vendors and schools reconstructs schools more as commercial outlets than places capable of helping their students make informed decisions about the new information technologies.

- Hamilton emphasises the importance of studying any tool in its context:

  > To examine a tool ... is to ask questions about the social and intentional relationships that it sustains. Just as we can learn much about ancient civilisation from its axe heads, cave paintings and grave markings, so we can also learn much about a modern pedagogy from its books, wall-charts, writing implements and architecture. (Hamilton 1987, pp.62–3)

Too often, discourses about the new information technologies and curriculum describe computer effects or outcomes from using them. Papert's (1987) concern about technocentric claims for computers or software echoes this point. Two hundred years from now, how much could be learned about Australian primary schooling by examining, for example, a Macintosh computer?

---

6   See, for instance, Wexler (1987) for a general argument and Bigum (1991) for an argument concerned specifically with computers in schools.

- Hamilton notes a long historical trend towards the greater deployment of educational materials:

    With the aid of technical devices, the transmission of experience has become more authentic (e.g. through the use of audio and video recording), more widespread (e.g. through the use of printing) and more rapid (e.g. through the use of communication satellites). (Hamilton 1987, p.63)

The authenticity of experience is highlighted by the use of new information technologies to prepare and transmit digital reproductions of text, voice and images. These data are sent in large volume and at high speed around the globe. The 'real' thing from which the digital copy was made tends to fade as the digital form is reproduced over and over and in some instances 'improved'.[7] Not only is this information decontextualised, but in many instances it is valued because the previously necessary human component has been discarded, leaving 'pure' information. Hence, in their digital forms text can be 'read' without being seen, music 'heard' without being listened to, and images 'seen' without being looked at. Only on some occasions is a decision made to open a window or ear for humans to see or hear what a machine 'sees' or 'hears' (and always at a necessarily lower resolution). For instance, in the 1990 Gulf War, the only need for the transmission of pictures back to a military base was to confirm that what the computer in a missile 'saw', using its eyeless 'vision', was a target recognisable by human sight. The role of the soldier was reduced to privileged voyeur, not controller of the line of flight.

- And, finally, Hamilton questions the claims commonly made on behalf of educational technologies—that they are good—by asking 'for whom?'

    The discourse of computers in schools is commonly based upon claims about the benefits of computers for learners. These claims and much of the technology to be found in classrooms have been traced by Douglas Noble (1988) to the research interests of the American military in training personnel to use complex weapons systems. This lineage of classroom educational technologies is important for the new information technologies generally. The discourse of the near-future new information technologies is silent on its military associations and is framed in terms of the 'important' task of building the ultimate interface for man and machine. The goal of perfecting the human–computer interface is never represented in terms of perfecting the interface of a killing machine with its user, and the fact that much of

---

7   For instance, digital recordings of music or scanned computer images of works of art are sometimes 'improved' in this sense.

the research funding and direction of the new information technologies is driven by military interests is seldom made clear. The implication of a deeply held belief in progress for its own sake[8] and the military interest of keeping one step ahead of your opponent, whether real or imagined, are also rarely debated.

There is evidence of a frustrated acceptance that some people will continue to determine what is 'good' for themselves despite the best efforts of cutting-edge development to continue to get more into a chip and to make interfaces more intuitive and on-line storage even more gargantuan by yesterday's standards. In a recent *Byte* forum on forecasting the next decade of technology, Alan Kay made this observation about the year 2000:

> One of the best predictions we can make is that there will still be lots of COBOL programmers. You just can't get rid of anything that's once worked. The style of interface I was associated with, the overlapping windows and all that stuff, I'm sure will still be there ... (quoted in Linderholm 1991, p.46)

The importance of asking about the interests represented in curriculum is a practice now well known to many teachers. Pursuing similar questions about the new information technologies and curriculum has often been stymied by the widespread acceptance of the acontexual, technocentric myth that computers are 'good for kids'.

Hamilton's very short contribution to the debate is useful because it underlines the significance of pursuing cultural analyses of curriculum as important bases for constructing different 'readings' of the new information technologies and curriculum.

Meighan and Reid's challenged schools
Though dated, a short speculative paper by Roland Meigan and William Reid (1982) is useful in drawing together more carefully reasoned arguments about the kinds of challenges schools face in an age in which information is plentiful and the social functions of schooling less certain. They suggest that the new information technologies represent a different kind of challenge to schooling than that represented by previous educational technologies. Adopting a Newtonian perspective on curriculum change by asking what makes curriculum so stable, rather than the usual (Aristotelian) question of what makes the curriculum change, they point to the institutionalisation of curriculum as the means by which schools have successfully weathered previous waves of educational technology and curriculum reform movements. They list four aspects of

---

8   A good discussion of the implication of the ideology of progress and computers in education can be found in Bromley (1992).

the social climate over the last century, in which curriculum has become institutionalised, as significant in terms of their socioeconomic analysis:

1 Schooling has been premised on an assumption that it would continue to grow 'to meet a dimly discerned future where its ultimate destiny and justification would lie' (Meigan & Reid 1982, p.354). The infrastructure of schooling has always been based upon some degree of expansion.

2 Society has given schools a monopoly on knowledge transmission.

3 Society-made schools were the only bridge for the passage from local to national identification.

4 Society-made schooling was the means for distributing each generation into occupations 'highly differentiated in terms of conditions of employment and financial and status rewards' (Meigan & Reid 1982, p.355).

Meigan and Reid argue that the elements of the environment that were so supportive of a stable curriculum are those most likely to be challenged by the new information technologies. In particular, they foresee a world moving from an energy-rich to an information-rich economy and the conditions for supporting schooling shifting in ways that may threaten the existence of schools as they are currently known. They point to shifts in each of these aspects of the current climate, some more related to the growth of the new information technologies than others.

With respect to the continuous growth of schooling, they note the increasing difficulty of sustaining labour-intensive activities and observe that many education systems are either in a steady state or contracting. More importantly, they argue, the rationale for expanding schooling based upon a 'dimly discerned future' is no longer believable. They argue that the combination of these two shifts will accelerate the decline of schooling. Interestingly, they identify these outcomes as being least implicated with the new information technologies.

The second shift that is identified is the increasing availability of high-quality information outside formal educational structures. It is a shift noted by Jean-François Lyotard (1984) in terms of what he calls an 'exteriorization of knowledge'; that is, a move from a period in which people and what they know are separated so that we are valued less for what we know and more because we know how to find out. Meigan and Reid point to the high quality and contemporary nature of video compared with school texts. They suggest that the home as a key site for the acquisition of high-technology products will inevitably become the focus for information access:

Here will be found information channels which are controllable, interactive, up-to-date and client oriented, while schools are starved of the funds necessary even to maintain their stocks of traditional textbooks. (Meigan & Reid 1982, pp.355–6)

The third shift, less directly described by Meigan and Reid, concerns the loss of the school's role as an agent of social integration. This is a development recently described by John Hinkson (1991). Meigan and Reid point to the shift in the availability of work due to the impact of the new information technologies and argue that the newly emerging service-related jobs are 'problematically related to conventional social class categories' (Meigan & Reid 1982, p.356).

The fourth shift, also identified by many commentators over the past decade, is the changes in the structures of occupations. Some changes of structure are so great that they effectively mean the loss of an occupation or the creation of a new one. In the face of the loss of large numbers of the occupations traditionally linked to particular forms of schooling, Meigan and Reid reason that students will find schools increasingly irrelevant to their employment needs and aspirations.

It is argued that these climate shifts, taken together, spell significant changes for schooling and the home. Optimistically, it is suggested that schools could surrender their knowledge-dissemination role and return to the traditional goals of a liberal education—that is, 'the development of wisdom, judgement, active intelligence and civic responsibility' (Meigan & Reid 1982, p.358).

Meigan and Reid's paper, although pre-dating the ones considered above, extends the frame or scope for thinking about the new information technologies and curriculum to include a consideration of the important social and economic changes that have accompanied the growth of computers and their related technologies in most aspects of contemporary society. The 'deschooling' theme that runs through their paper has much in common with Papert's (1980) famous polemic. Like Papert, Meigan and Reid identify the structural features of schooling as the means by which curriculum has been so resistant to change; unlike Papert, their analysis makes an attempt to identify the larger cultural forces at work. The next section attempts to extend the arguments further by considering cultural shifts on an even larger scale. In doing so it is possible to map some of these more locally based accounts onto this larger picture.

Doll's postmodern curriculum
In a range of public, academic and cultural discourses, it is hard not to notice the common use of the term 'postmodern', often in association with particular social practices and products.[9] Employing the prefix 'post' ensures an implied reference to something that has gone before, in this

9   There has been, for instance, an advertisement for postmodern soup in the *Australian Women's Weekly*.

case the 'modern'. Relying upon time as a means of distinguishing the modern and the postmodern, however, is fraught with difficulty. The term has been used so widely to refer to social practices in so many diverse fields in such a range of times this century that attempts at periodisation inevitably fail and, say some, cloud meanings that do not rely upon the identification of time scales. Nevertheless, many definitions find it hard to escape the implicit temporal dimension of the term. Stephen Toulmin's claim is a case in point. He attempted something of a definition when he wrote *we no longer live in the "modern" world*, but rather in a 'postmodern world ... the world that has not yet discovered how to define itself in terms of what it *is*, but only in terms of what it has *just-now-ceased to be*' (Toulmin 1982, p.254).

In an age of obsessive age labelling, often involving the use of the prefix 'post', it might be said that the labelling itself represents a kind of cultural uncertainty on a large scale, almost a sense that we had better have a label to describe what we think is happening in case it actually does. The rise of uncertainty in a number of cultural spheres is an important element in postmodernism. It is one of the ideas on which William Doll (1989) draws in his exoteric account of postmodern curriculum.

Doll draws on contemporary (postmodern) science in considering the metaphorical and literal implications for curriculum of post-Newtonian views of the physical universe. Newton, here, is employed as a symbol of the rise of modern science in the seventeenth century. It was a science that was one of the early claimants to being a 'theory of everything'. Its claims are indicated by this quotation from the French mathematician Laplace:

> An intelligence knowing, at any given instant of time, all forces acting in nature, as well as the momentary positions of all things of which the universe consists, would be able to comprehend the motions of the largest bodies of the world and those of the smallest atoms in one single formula, provided it were sufficiently powerful to subject all data to analysis; to it, nothing would be uncertain, both future and past would be present before its eyes. (quoted in Davies & Brown 1988, p.3)

While the limitations of this science have long been recognised and only survive in their pure form in school texts, the cultural influences of a predictable and controllable universe remain. Doll argues that the influences of Newtonian science are evident in the practices of schooling and focuses his attention on curriculum by drawing heavily upon Ilya Prigogine's Nobel Prize–winning work on the thermodynamics of far-from-equilibrium systems.

The significance of Doll's work is not the outcomes, which can be mapped onto existing liberal and emancipatory views about education, but the fact that the metaphors he applies are derived from contemporary (postmodern) views of science.[10] This contrasts with current school curricula which, claims Doll, have their roots in the Newtonian paradigm that dominated Western scientific and intellectual thought well into this century. While science has moved well beyond this paradigm, social sciences that have been founded in this model, particularly education, have been unmoved:

> The abandonment of Newtonian mechanics for understanding reality is relatively well advanced. Yet, the metaphysical view of the world it once inspired has proved rather more durable. Perhaps because of cultural lag, only in recent decades have the philosophical implications of quantum physics begun to reverberate through other knowledge domains. Overall, the new image of reality unfolded by modern science portends a radical revision of how the world and human consciousness itself is to be comprehended. (Lucas 1985, p.65)

The certainty, predictability, control and instrumental rationality that characterise the Newtonian paradigm makes a stark contrast with what Frederick Ferré has labelled 'postmodern science' (quoted in Toulmin 1982, p.210). Ilya Prigogine and Isabelle Stengers capture the spirit of postmodern science this way:

> Our vision of nature is undergoing a radical change toward the multiple, the temporal, and the complex. For a long time a mechanistic world view dominated Western science. In this view the world appeared as a vast automaton. We now understand that we live in a pluralistic world. (Prigogine & Stengers 1984, p.xxvii)

> We were seeking general all-embracing schemes that could be expressed in terms of eternal laws, but we have found time, events, evolving particles. We were also searching for symmetry, and here also we were surprised, since we discovered symmetry-breaking processes on all levels, from elementary particles up to biology and ecology. (Prigogine & Stengers 1984, p.292)

Doll describes the work of Prigogine that is the basis for his curriculum analysis:

> Prigogine received the 1977 Nobel Prize in Chemistry for his work on dissipative or far-from-equilibrium thermodynamic structures. A far-from-equilibrium structure is one in the process of becoming, such as in a basin of water when the hot and the cold are beginning to merge and blend. Structures of this sort characterize chemistry and biology. They become the very essence of living systems. They are not the

---

10   In fact, he claims that studying contemporary developments in biology, chemistry, cognition, literary theory, mathematics and theology is a must for curricularists (Doll 1989, p.251).

physical, inert, mechanical structures Newton used in his *Principia*.
(Doll 1989, p.44)

Prigogine believes that dissipative, *becoming* structures are far more common than equilibrium, *being* structures, and therefore, argues Doll, dissipative structures rather than equilibrium structures should be studied as a foundational model for curriculum. Doll takes three aspects of dissipative structures and develops implications for curriculum:

1   the nature of open (as opposed to closed) systems;

2   the structure of complexity (as opposed to simplicity); and

3   transformatory (as opposed to accumulative) change.

I will use this framework as a basis for further elaboration of the new information technologies and curriculum.

The new information technologies and (post?)modern curriculum

John von Neumann's name is associated with the architecture of most modern digital computers.[11] The von Neumann machine is the archetypal Newtonian machine; it obeys prescribed rules, processing data in a totally predictable (programmed) manner. It is an icon for the controllable, predictable universe of Laplace and has become a significant metaphor for educational practice (Stern 1992).

A machine becoming metaphorically significant is one thing, but it seems odd that schools should actually seek to acquire them when they had not bothered to acquire significant numbers of other machines, particularly those that have proliferated since the Industrial Revolution. Part of the explanation may lie in the nature of the computer as machine. As a machine, the computer is different from the machines that can trace their ancestry back to steam engines and spinning wheels. Apart from controlling mechanical devices, a computer does no work in the way that steam engines and spinning wheels do. As David Bolter argues:

> In that respect the machine [computer] is an extension of the mechanical rather than the dynamic aspect of Western European technology, of the clock rather than the steam engine. The clock provided information more conveniently and eventually more accurately than the sundial had before, but it did not intrude physically

---

11   In recent years the limitations imposed by von Neumann architecture has seen the design and development of different architectures, commonly involving some form of parallel processing, i.e. lots of von Neumann machines running in parallel—see, for instance, Hillis (1992).

upon life except by ringing the hour. The usefulness of its information was perhaps not obvious; improved information is seldom as obviously useful as tangible improvements such as a better plow or a more efficient loom. Like early computers, early clocks were expensive and delicate, and it required a major corporate effort to acquire one. As clocks became more common, however, they became not merely useful but unavoidable. Men and women began to work, eat, and sleep by the clock, and as soon as they decided to regulate their actions by this arbitrary measurer of time, the clock was transformed from an expression of civic pride into a necessity of urban life. (Bolter 1984, p.38)

The family resemblance to clocks goes some way, then, to help locate the appeal of computers for schools. Parallels and resonances with curriculum are strong. The modern curriculum can be seen as a kind of program that runs (on) by a clock. The appeal of a machine that makes no apparent change to the physical environment, offers a clocklike, predictable and infinitely repeatable regularity in its operation, and raises measured time to an even greater significance has obvious appeal for a curriculum premised on control, predictability and Newtonian time.[12] More importantly, the computer, like the clock, quickly became a symbol of status, signifying that the owner operated according to the rhythm of the new technology (clock or computer). To own a clock or a computer, then, (was) is to participate in progress, to affirm Newtonian time, an abstract measure of the passing of experience that has no end and no beginning. An ahistorical, linear time is a characteristic of a closed system, one of the elements in Doll's account of curriculum.

Open v. closed systems
A closed system in thermodynamics is one which exchanges energy but not matter with its environment. Such systems have no history; they are inert, 'immortal', and capable of indefinite maintenance without further interaction with their environment. As Doll argues, such systems are tightly controlled, have few variables, have their parameters preset, and exhibit high predictability. Open systems, on the other hand, exchange energy and matter with their environment, and as Prigogine and Stengers (1984, p.127) point out, 'they exist only because they are open'; furthermore, 'they feed on the flux of matter and energy coming to them from the outside world'.

Computers are by their nature incomplete machines. They are made whole through programming. They can also be interactive machines, in which case the total system is part human. Humans understood as imperfect machines add a dimension of openness and complexity to the system that designers of software work hard to minimise. Much of the importance of minimising human imperfection in using a machine

---

12 Time that is abstract and 'equably flowing', independent of anything that is external (Newton quoted in Bolter 1984, p.108).

derives from the interests of the US military in designing human interfaces for increasingly complex weapons systems (Noble 1988, 1989).

The problem of human–machine communication is one which attracts a large research effort. Most of this research sees the problem in terms of making software easier to use, smarter, or friendlier, and is premised upon a faith that the ultimate mousetrap can in fact be built—that is, that machine–human communication can be perfected. There are views that deny this possibility,[13] but the dominant position is that the computer, the ultimate closed system, can be so designed to interact perfectly with an open system, a human. Recently, it has been suggested that the problem lies not with making the computer more adapted to human needs but with adapting humans to computer requirements, and the term 'intelligent artificiality' (IA) has been coined to describe such understandings.[14]

Less predictable and determined views are also evident in the discourse of human–machine communication. For instance, in an interview for *Byte* magazine Ted Nelson, the inventor of hypertext, talks in terms of what he calls 'virtuality':

> The real problem is that the design of software virtuality, as I prefer to say, is an extremely complex, aesthetic design issue—and universally confused with a technical issue. In other words, I hold that the design of software is intrinsically a branch of cinema. Motion pictures are events on the screen that affect the mind and heart of the viewer. Software is events on the screen that affect the mind and the heart of the viewer, *with* interaction. So the only difference is that interaction is possible, so you have extended cinema in which the user exerts a certain measure of control.
>
> Now, *virtuality* is my term for the most important defining traits of software. Other people say things like *interface*, and to me the entire issue is one of virtuality. Virtuality is essentially the seeming of something as distinct from its reality, which is the nuts and bolts of the hardware. So everything has a virtuality, and you either design it explicitly or you do not ...
>
> A movie's virtuality is the conceptual structure and feel of that movie. So, the conceptual structure is the script and the characters, and the feel is the *mise-en-scène*, the atmosphere, the feelings that go with different scenes. And these are highly arbitrary and idiosyncratic and basically controlled by the director with great difficulty in the creation of the motion picture. So, that's where the distinction between conceptual structure and feel is for a movie.
>
> The conceptual structure of all automobiles is the same. They go left and right, forward and back, fast and slow, and there is very little beyond that. But the feel of automobiles is very different, and that is why automobiles have such variety.

13 See, for example, Suchman (1987).
14 It was reported that an advertisement on a local Melbourne radio station was seeking secretaries who are 'fully compatible with PC word processors'.

So, what I claim is that the conceptual structure and feel is the heart of a lot of things, but it is certainly the heart of software design. The conceptual structure is arbitrary, and the feel is very hard to control. (quoted in Linderholm 1991, p.42)

The discourse of the new information technologies and curriculum has little capacity to describe human–machine interaction in these terms. In Nelson's terms, the conceptual structure is all important. All too often the human 'feel' is dismissed as an imperfection which can be solved in terms of better conceptual structures. 'Feel' is not the kind of thing that can be easily programmed, controlled or predicted, and hence it sits outside the major discourses of the new information technologies. The computer is discursively constructed as an exemplar of the Newtonian paradigm, perfectly controlled and predictable, with little or no room for aesthetic notions like 'feel'. It is at this juncture that the question of whether or not a machine can teach crystallises.

A device like a computer can be seen as a perfect closed system, ideally suited to support and maintain a modern curriculum, characterised by preset ends and controlled by a feedback loop that adjusts the delivery of instruction in order to achieve its ends. The failure of software that is specifically designed for this purpose can be seen as a particular instance of the general problem of using machines to control and direct humans. The irony of using the ultimate, modern machine, the Dream of Reason, to support curriculum that supposedly is taking students into a postmodern world is lost on those trapped in their Newtonian time machines.

It is not only instructional software that so neatly fits the closed-system metaphor. All software used in schools is commonly characterised by a form of closed-system understanding. There is a tendency to make assumptions about the system; that is, that student and software together constitute a closed system. The decontextualised claims that software X will teach skill Y are indicative of this view. What Papert (1987) has termed 'technocentrism' comes from understandings that are consistent with the logic of closed simple systems—that is, that causes and effects can be predicted and understood. What is ignored is that learning cannot be understood solely in terms of a closed system. Learning is *situated*. Contemporary views on pedagogy regard 'activity' and 'situations' as integral to learning.[15] Teachers report a sense of how open most learning 'systems' are when they take the time to observe carefully students using software.[16] What they report is far removed from the decontextualised claims for software made by vendors, claims that celebrate a modern machine in a modern curriculum.

While it is easy to identify software, computing practices and curricula that resemble closed systems, it is more difficult to identify computing practices in schools that might resemble Prigogine's open, dissipative

---

15 See, for example, Brown, Collins and Duguid (1989).
16 Bigum and Gilding (1985) report a video technique that captures the use of software by students.

structures. There is, however, an interesting and important practice resembling such structures that is characteristic of the work of computing professionals.

At both a local and a global level, computing is remarkable for its reliance upon an open, human network of information exchange to support its practice. In this network, people cope with the complexity and unpredictability of developments and problems in hardware, software and systems by obtaining help on a need-to-know basis. At a global level the human network is supported by a communications network based on university computers in most countries of the world. At this level the system is certainly complex and supports not only electronic mail but an enormous number of newsgroups or electronic bulletin boards, and scholarly lists. Newsgroups and lists come and go according to the needs and interests of the system. Links are made between professionals on the basis of problems to be solved and generally disappear when the need for further communication ceases—that is, structure emerges and dissolves as the activity patterns of the community evolve. This self-organisational aspect of the network maps neatly onto Prigogine's dissipative, self-organising structures.

There are no equivalent practices in schools, apart from the extent to which teachers engaged in computing participate in a local or extended support network of computer users. While there is some informal recounting of classroom behaviour (that is, students constructing informal support networks of their own) that maps onto the practices of computing professionals, there has been little attempt to describe systematically a pedagogy that supports such student activity. It usually attracts a pragmatic response by teachers as being helpful in coping with the use of computers in their classroom. Dissipative, self-organising moments in classrooms are probably more common than might be imagined. They tend not to be seen when so much of curriculum discourse is framed in terms of closed, linear and predictable systems.

The simple (and separate) v. the complex (and cosmological)
Newton's world was one of order, harmony and simplicity. Linear equations accounted for a simple, ordered reality that could be observed objectively.[17] Prigogine, on the other hand, posits a science in which complexity is the dominant feature. The linearity of cause and effect in simple, near-equilibrium, closed systems, in which a small perturbation causes a small effect, can be contrasted with complex, open systems in which a small perturbation may have very large effects or no effect at all.

Using Doll's analysis of current curricula as closed systems for the moment, it is possible to 'read' the more or less predictable and small changes in curriculum arising from the small perturbation corresponding to introducing computers into the curriculum. The revolutionary claims made on behalf of introducing the new information technologies into the curriculum are flawed if curricula can be best described in terms of simple,

---

17 Before Heisenberg and Einstein, it was believed that observer effects could be eliminated.

closed systems. In a sense, some of the projects that have involved saturating schools or parts of schools with the new information technologies[18] appear to acknowledge this; that is, that the only way to see the expected large outcomes is to employ a large perturbation. As in most technology-driven experiments in schools, the curriculum is taken as a given, and it is assumed that it can be changed. If Doll is correct and school curricula are best understood as closed, near-equilibrium systems, then these systems are characterised by being particularly good at retaining their equilibrium; that is, they absorb almost any amount of change with internal adjustments.

As Roy Pea and Karen Sheingold, among others, have described, this perspective on curriculum also allows a somewhat different interpretation of the property of computing technology to *reflect* :

> ... we have continually found that educational technologies serve as mirrors of minds and the cultures in which they 'live'. Rather than radically amplifying or transforming the processes of teaching and learning, as many predicted, they instead reflect the expectancies represented in classrooms and the knowledge and skills of individuals using them. (Pea & Sheingold 1987, p.x)

The 'reflection' of curriculum rather than its 'transformation' may be attributable to the ready absorption by the curriculum (a near-equilibrium, simple system) of the new information technologies (the perturbation). The change quickly becomes a part of the system to be changed and takes on its attributes. What occurs may be more akin to *colonisation* than *reflection*. If this account is developed, it is interesting to ask what curricula are well reflected and what curricula are poorly reflected. The latter category may offer examples of curricula that are complex and further from equilibrium than most school curricula.

The attributes of simplicity and complexity described by Doll are similar to those described by Toulmin as 'separate' and 'cosmological'. Toulmin notes that Western scientific enquiry up to the seventeenth-century could be described as highly interconnected or cosmological, and that

> from the early seventeenth century on, and increasingly so as the centuries passed, the tasks of scientific inquiry were progressively divided up between separate and distinct 'disciplines'. (Toulmin 1982, p.228)

Such practices lead to what Toulmin calls a 'spectator view' of science, knowledge and teaching. It is a view that most subject-specific software dutifully reproduces. It is not hard to find instances of software in schools

---

18 So-called schools of the future projects, like Hennigen in Boston and the Sunrise schools in Australia, are typical of this kind of approach.

which conveys and supports an understanding of the separateness of knowledge. The dearth of software that might support a more holistic view of knowledge leads us to ask if it is possible to have 'cosmological' software with current computing technology, and if so, what would it look like?

The emergence of various forms of *hypertext* points to the capacity of the new information technologies to support a low level of interconnectedness of information. This technical connectivity ought not to be confused with the kind of cosmological connectivity to which Toulmin refers. Nevertheless, as a metaphor for the idea, hypertext is an interesting contrast to the educational software that celebrates the separateness of knowledge. It should also be noted that, for some time, the computing industry has been moving from the promotion of separate, stand-alone microcomputers to microcomputers that are connected. While the early connectivity of such networks was designed to support simple exchanges of information, there is an emerging effort to develop software that supports group work and, beyond that, to connect all users of computers to 'all' information sources in ways that employ 'intelligent' agents to seek out information on behalf of particular users. While all of these developments are interesting, none approaches the kind of holistic ways of knowing to which Toulmin refers.

Transformative v. incremental change

Education is concerned with change;[19] as Doll (1989, p.249) puts it, 'directed purposive, intentional change'. Notions of curriculum change draw upon broad cultural notions of social change, which in turn can be traced back to the linear science of the seventeenth century. Linear equations characterised the birth of modern science in the 1600s. Their great virtue was that they were able to be solved, and their non-linear counterparts generally were not. It mattered little how much of the world might be described as linear; the important thing was that results could be obtained. In this context nonlinear systems were seen to be something of an abberration, a deviation from the linear norm. You can still find the influence of this effect in most physics texts, where treatment of nonlinear systems, if they are treated at all, appears in an appendix. The cultural implications of chosing to work with linear systems would have been much fewer if, in fact, much of the world was well described by straight lines and linear equations. However, as Stanislaw Ulam is reported to have remarked, 'to call the study of chaos "nonlinear science" was like calling zoology "the study of nonelephant animals" ' (quoted in Gleick 1988, p.68).

It is from linear or straight-line science that understandings of the proportionality of cause and effect can be traced; that is, to effect a particular change you need a particular-sized cause. While this works more

---

19 Indeed, since the arrival of computers in schools, change has taken on new meanings derived from the rhetoric of the distributors of the new information technologies: change is about changing yesterday's computer model for tomorrow's model.

or less well for two billiard balls and to some extent for larger objects like planets, it is hopelessly inadequate for more complex systems. Importantly, the nature of change in simple, linear systems is incremental. Change really amounts to shifting the balance of variables within well-defined limits. The discourse of curriculum change commonly restates this view by using terms like 'improve', 'enhance', 'enrich', 'evolve', 'develop', 'encourage', 'foster' and 'perfect'. That is not to say that improvement, enhancement etc. are not worthwhile educational goals, but the assumption that underpins each is that this kind of change occurs more like the incremental, linear change of modern science than the spontaneous, discontinuous and erratic change that derives from nonlinear accounts of physical reality. The use of computers in classrooms has also been discursively framed in transformational terms[20] but, as with its non-computer-based cousins, change is still seen as linear and incremental. This kind of classroom use of computers and their related technologies is affirmed in discourses which talk in terms of *integration* into the curriculum. The important thing is to keep things more or less as they are. As Doll puts it:

> In Newton's ideal universe, stability, not change, was the desired goal; change occurred rarely—and then was the result of a flaw in the universe which God as *Deus ex machina* put right by direct intervention. (Doll 1989, p.249)

In modern curriculum terms flaws are too often things to be corrected, to be erased, deviations from the ideal, even regarded as monsters! From a nonlinear or postmodern perspective, as Doll describes it, curriculum flaws and errors are the source of growth, of transformation, and have the capacity to bring about change on a large scale. This characteristic is more easily identified in the study of chaos in nonlinear dynamic systems, in which feedback of output back into input is the basis for the complex behaviour of such systems and accounts for small perturbations being multiplied rapidly to cause disproportionately large changes.[21] Computers are, of course, eminently suitable for modelling such systems and are the basis by which nonlinear systems can be investigated. It is therefore ironic to find such technology being used in classrooms to create simple, one-stage feedback loops, of the kind, 'you are wrong, try again!'

At least one discursive positioning of the new information technologies in education exploits the nonlinear science account of errors. Papert's (1980) elaboration of the philosophy of Logo identifies 'bugs' and the feedback loop entered into by 'debugging' as an essential component of the kind of learning environment for which he argues. Programming in any language provides many instances of the punctuational and

---

20   For instance, by Papert (1980).
21   The so-called butterfly effect is a case in point. The flapping of a butterfly's wings in Perth might multiply through the complex weather systems so that by the time it gets to Melbourne it is a wind storm.

transformative opportunities of bugs. The complexity of almost all programming tasks makes it virtually impossible for the programmer to anticipate the final outcome, and even when the kind of top-down planning which is valorised by the discourse of computer science education achieves a planned outcome, the outcome itself invariably suggests other programming changes or sometimes entirely new ways of tackling the problem. The mythology of computer programming being a rational and planned activity is questioned by the recent work of Sherry Turkle and Seymour Papert (1990) and, earlier, by the work of Suchman (1987). Suchman's work on plans and what she terms 'situated actions' resonates with the analysis Doll (1989, p.250) makes of the modern curriculum in terms of critiquing the traditional Tyler-Hunter model in which ends and the means to them are precisely described.

Suchman builds a strong case in favour of reversing the ontology of plans and actions. She argues that plans are the means by which we make sense of our actions and not, as many suppose, the basis for action. Her work, developed from George Herbert Mead's account of action, links at least two of the ideas that derive from nonlinear science or chaos. The importance of the 'situatedness' of action maps onto Prigogine's interest in open systems. Suchman's debunking of the significance of planning coincides with the determined unpredictability of most natural systems. She writes:

> Plans and accounts are distinguished from action as such by the fact that, to represent our actions, we must in some way make an object of them. Consequently, our descriptions of our actions come always before or after the fact, in the form of imagined projections and recollected reconstructions. (Suchman 1987, p.51)

In this context the notion of a planned curriculum takes on a very different appearance from its appearance if it were taken in a cultural context underpinned by the assumptions of Newtonian science. It would then seem that adding computers and their related technologies to the curriculum can be taken in two ways: either it is a perturbation to which the curriculum is adjusted (integrating computers across the curriculum),[22] or it is used to meet broad educational goals, in which computers represent a kind of beginning, a deliberate perturbation, an opening up of ideas and issues concerning the new information technologies in education and society more generally. In the former model, the curriculum effectively ensures that newer forms of the technology can be similarly absorbed. The balance of the curriculum is only shifted in a small way and, if they have any effect at all, computers now contribute to the continued stability of the curriculum.

More importantly, it can be argued that, in blindly pursuing the development of a modern curriculum with the ultimate, modern machine,

---

22 Not unlike other educational technology perturbations, such as television and film; see the account of Cuban's work above.

schools have ensured that their contribution to preparing students to participate in the important debates about the place of the new information technologies in society is irrelevant at best, and, at worst, complicit in providing a smokescreen for the social acceptance of the new information technologies. At a time in which computing and communication technologies are being employed to reshape our world in ways that few currently apprehend, schools have opted to appear 'busy' by employing computers to maintain a curriculum that derives from an earlier age, when factories and assembly lines were significant cultural metaphors, when Newtonian time was the only way to think about time, and when the world was a much more certain place.

Conclusion

This brief exercise in applying ideas taken from postmodern science to curriculum and the new information technologies suggests that, rather than moving schools into some new information age, computing lends support to the maintenance of a modern curriculum, a curriculum that is founded upon a Newtonian paradigm of science, a curriculum that looks back to past ways of knowing the world and acting upon it. It seems incongruous that schools should recite the claim that they need computers in order to prepare their students for an information or postmodern age when the technology is being used to maintain a resilient, modern curriculum.

References

Bigum, C. (1991), 'Schools for cyborgs: Educating aliens', in *ACEC '91, Proceedings of the Ninth Australian Computers in Education Conference*, Computer Education Group of Queensland, Brisbane.

Bigum, C.J. & Gilding, A. (1985), 'A video monitoring technique for investigating computer-based learning programs', *Computers & Education*, no.9, pp.95–9.

Bolter, J.D. (1984), *Turing's Man: Western Culture in the Computer Age*, University of North Carolina Press, Chapel Hill.

Bowers, C.A. (1988), *The Cultural Dimensions of Educational Computing: Understanding the Non-neutrality of Technology*, Teachers College Press, New York.

Bromley, H. (1992), 'Culture, power and educational computing', in C. Bigum & B. Green (eds), *Understanding the New Information Technologies in Education: A Resource for Teachers*, Centre for Studies in Information Technologies and Education, Deakin University, Geelong, Vic.

Brown, J.S., Collins, A. & Duguid, P. (1989), 'Situated cognition and the culture of learning', *Educational Researcher*, vol.18, no.1, pp.32–42.

Cuban, L. (1986), *Teachers and Machines: The Classroom Use of Technology since 1920*, Teachers College Press, New York.

Davies, P.C.W. & Brown, J. (1988), *Superstrings: A Theory of Everything?*, Cambridge University Press, Cambridge.

Doll, W.E. Jr (1989), 'Foundations for a post-modern curriculum', *Journal of Curriculum Studies*, vol.21, no.3, pp.243–53.

Dupuy, J.-P. (1980), 'Myths of the informational society', in K. Woodward (ed.), *The Myths of Information: Technology and Postindustrial Culture*, Coda Press, Madison, Wis.

Gleick, J. (1988), *Chaos: Making a New Science*, Sphere Books, London.

Hamilton, D. (1987), *Education: An Unfinished Curriculum*, Department of Education, University of Glasgow, Glasgow.

Hillis, W. D. (1992), 'What is massively parallel computing, and why is it important?', *Daedalus*, vol.121, no.1, pp.1–16.

Hinkson, J. (1991), *Postmodernity: State and Education*, ESA844 Administrative Context of Schooling, Deakin University, Geelong, Vic.

Linderholm, O. (1991), 'Mind melding: How far can the human/computer interface go?', *Byte*, vol.16, no.11, pp.41–6.

Lucas, C. (1985), 'Out at the edge: Notes on a paradigm shift', *Journal of Counseling and Development*, vol.64, no.3, pp.165–72.

Lyotard, J.-F. (1984), *The Postmodern Condition: A Report on Knowledge*, trans. G. Bennington & B. Massumi, University of Minnesota Press, Minneapolis.

Meighan, R. & Reid, W. (1982), 'How will the "new technology" change the curriculum?', *Journal of Curriculum Studies*, vol.14, no 4, pp.353–8.

Noble, D.D. (1988), 'Education, technology, and the military', in L.E. Beyer & M.W. Apple (eds), *The Curriculum: Problems, Politics, and Possibilities*, State University of New York Press, Albany, NY.

Noble, D.D. (1989), 'Mental materiel: The militarization of learning and intelligence in US education', in K. Robins & L. Levidow (eds), *Cyborg Worlds: The Military Information Society*, Free Association Press, London

Papert, S. (1972), 'Teaching children thinking', *Mathematics Teaching*, no.58, Spring, pp.2–7.

Papert, S. (1980), *Mindstorms: Children, Computers and Powerful Ideas*, Basic Books, New York.

Papert, S. (1987), 'Computer criticism vs. technocentric thinking', *Educational Researcher*, vol.16, no.1, pp.22–30.

Pea, R.D. & Sheingold, K. (1987), *Mirrors of Minds: Patterns of Experience in Educational Computing*, Ablex, Norwood, NJ.

Prigogine, I. & Stengers, I. (1984), *Order out of Chaos: Man's New Dialogue with Nature*, Heinemann, London.

Schostak, J.F. (1988a), 'Introduction', in J.F. Schostak (ed.), *Breaking into the Curriculum: The Impact of Information Technology on Schooling*, Methuen, London.

Schostak, J.F. (1988b), 'The Jet Set Willy curriculum', in J.F. Schostak (ed.), *Breaking into the Curriculum: The Impact of Information Technology on Schooling*, Methuen, London.

Schostak, J.F. (1988c), 'Secondary schooling—the sense of an ending', in J.F. Schostak (ed.), *Breaking into the Curriculum: The Impact of Information Technology on Schooling*, Methuen, London.

Stern, N. (1992), 'Editible selves: Thought-experiments with information technology', in C. Bigum & B. Green (eds), *Understanding the New Information Technologies in Education: A Resource for Teachers*, Centre for Studies in Information Technologies and Education, Deakin University, Geelong, Vic.

Suchman, L.A. (1987), *Plans and Situated Actions: The Problem of Human–Machine Communication*, Cambridge University Press, Cambridge.

Toulmin, S. (1982), *The Return to Cosmology: Postmodern Science and the Theology of Nature*, University of California Press, Berkeley & Los Angeles.

Turkle, S. & Papert, S. (1990), 'Epistemological pluralism: Styles and voices within the computer culture', *Signs*, vol.16 no.1 pp.128–57.

Wexler, P. (1987), *Social Analysis of Education: After the New Sociology*, Routledge & Kegan Paul, London.

Winner, L. (1989), 'Mythinformation in the high-tech era', in T. Forester (ed.), *Computers in the Human Context: Information Technology, Productivity, and People*, Basil Blackwell, Oxford.

Part III

Framing textual practice

Ian Reid

An attitude of suspicion towards abstractly formulated notions can be healthy. Why use a term such as 'textual practice'? For despite its gesture towards actual, tangible human activities, it may appear to lack precise conceptual focus—to be mere jargon for plain old reading and writing. Should we not stick to simple words to describe simple phenomena? The answer is twofold: first, what is often taken to be plain old reading and writing has never been as simple as it seemed, and needs especially to be better theorised in relation to curriculum framing; second, 'reading' and 'writing' are not altogether what they used to be, and renaming can help to emphasise the technological nature of the change they have undergone. In my remarks here on textual practice, I begin by considering a few educational aspects of *textuality* and then go on to say a little about the related concept of *framing* and its practical relevance to classroom behaviour.

Textuality and literacy

At the outset we can conveniently remind ourselves of the argument advanced by Jean-François Lyotard (1984) in his book *The Postmodern Condition: A Report on Knowledge.* Lyotard sees 'modern' thought as having been supported by certain kinds of myth or philosophical arch-narrative, which cannot now be considered legitimate. Their two main versions are the political 'story' of enlightened progress towards a just society and the scientific 'story' of an epistemological unity 'that links the sciences together as moments in the becoming of spirit' (Lyotard 1984, p.33). Disbelief in those arch-narratives is what defines, for Lyotard, our postmodern condition. Social action and intellectual enquiry, no longer structured by such grandly dogmatic sanctions, turn instead to fragmentary mini-narratives. Science must legitimate itself on its own performative terms. Larger ethical imperatives are taken over by the state and the multinational corporation, and knowledge becomes a service industry, a commodified and instrumentalised technology of information.

Although those general observations are hardly new in themselves, their implications for language-based forms of learning are perhaps not yet widely understood. Linguistics and curriculum theory need to keep conferring, for example, about the ways in which the genres of narrative and argument may be changing, and about whether they are involved in a move towards something like a 'postmodern pedagogy'. Consider one issue: how does the technologisation of knowledge affect the traditional opposition between speech and writing? It has been customary in our culture to distinguish sharply between spoken and written modes; and the latter mode has normally counted as 'text'. Some theorists, for instance Paul Ricoeur (1981), still see an act of speech as belonging to a particular interlocutory situation, addressed to someone directly and dialogically, whereas writing is supposed to be an autonomous entity, separated from the occasion of its utterance and available to anyone who can read. But as John Thompson points out, this contrast is hardly adequate in an age of electronic communication, when 'speech can be recorded and transcribed and ... "inscription" can assume many different forms' (Thompson 1984, p.197). Not only is it now possible for oral utterances to be relayed to huge audiences, stored, edited, packaged and so on, but conversely written texts do not stand outside the conditions of dialogic discourse: they anticipate particular readerships, shape themselves therefore as objects for consumption, and indeed in some of their most recent electronic forms (notably interactive videodisks) are directly conversational.

Technological developments today move so fast that their capacity to transform the very meaning of literacy keeps acquiring different dimensions. To mention just one instance: much current thinking about implications for the curriculum of the advent of personal computers assumes that keyboarding skills will be increasingly important; but suppose we are very close to an entirely new technological revolution whereby word processing can be simply voice-generated: what would that mean for literacy education? At any rate, the relations between speech and writing are radically unstable, and if any idea of a postmodern pedagogy is to be more than a facile and trendy slogan it must confront that instability in textual practices.

In a recent article called 'The electronic word: Literary study and the digital revolution', Richard Lanham suggests that the full significance of our word-processing technology has yet to be grasped by most of us who use personal computers merely as 'handy engines to produce printed texts about printed texts' (Lanham 1989, p.265). What the electronic word has actually brought into being, he argues, is the capacity for truly interactive reader response, and it thus materially deconstructs the opposition between 'creative' and 'critical writing' as texts change in their passage from one screen and keyboard to another. Lanham goes so far as to insist that this electronic proliferation of textuality has profound implications for the whole world of writing, publishing and 'literature', not least for legal concepts such as authorial rights:

> If 'textbooks' are distributed via local area networks, telephone lines, or more capacious broadband conduits of some sort, how will we protect the intellectual property of those who have created these

110

works? And if the works are excerpted and revised continually by those using them, as we know they will be, who will then 'own' the revised property then redistributed for yet further revision? Who will 'own' an interactive novel after it has been repeatedly interacted with? (Lanham 1989, pp.280–1)

There may be an element of hyperbole here; but Lanham goes on to say that in any case the very idea of 'publication' is sure to change as we incorporate into texts not only commentaries but also responses, and responses to responses: we will then be moving, as he puts it, 'from a series of orations to a continuing conversation and, as we have always known, these two rhetorics differ fundamentally' (Lanham 1989, p.284). He predicts that electronic technology will serve to reactivate an education based on *rhetoric*—not, of course, in the attenuated sense of a merely taxonomic obsession with tropes but in the larger sense of a training in the compositional arts of powerful language. As far as my own field of literary pedagogy is concerned, Lanham's message about the impact of technological developments is this: 'We must take into our own disciplinary domain the world of general literacy upon which literature depends' (Lanham 1989, p.288).

Robert Scholes (1987) has argued along similar lines, though without specific reference to electronic technology, in a paper on the relevance of textuality to literature and literacy teaching. Indeed, he urges teachers of English:

> to set aside the notion of *literature* and centre teaching around the related but distinct notion of *textuality* for the following reasons. First, *literature* implies purely verbal, written texts only, ruling out oral, visual, musical and mixed media. Second, *literature* implies classic or great works only, ruling out more modest texts and discouraging active, critical engagement with the masterpieces presented for study ... Thirdly, *literature* implies imaginative or fictional texts only, ruling out essays, speeches and the many forms of investigative, analytical, and persuasive textuality that are so important in our culture. The teaching of *literature*, in short, depends upon so many exclusions that it leaves its practitioners cut off from most of the textual practices that are presently active and influential in óur world. (Scholes 1987, pp.73–4)

More than a rhetorical aspect of language, textuality is to be regarded, according to Scholes's (somewhat loose) definition, as a human capacity— as literacy in its critical dimension.[1] Whereas literacy usually signifies, he says, 'minimal competence in handling the printed word: just enough skill to be manipulated by written texts' (Scholes 1987, p.74), *textuality* can signify not simply 'a higher degree of skill than that of mere literacy, but the ability to detect the mechanisms of manipulation at work in text and

---

1   Bill Green (1988b) has some interesting remarks on 'critical literacy', in a paper commissioned by the Education Department of Western Australia.

to enjoy the play of manipulative forces' (Scholes 1987, p.75). Since the study of figurative language will be important for this purpose, texts of the sort usually regarded as literary will remain important also; but 'persuasive and argumentative texts of all sorts' should come under the same scrutiny.

This increasing emphasis on textuality is by no means confined to the humanities field. It has just as much relevance, I suggest, to scientific and technological education. A useful point of reference here is a debate in the pages of a book that I edited several years ago, *The Place of Genre in Learning* (Reid 1987). In their contributions, John Dixon and Frances Christie put forward different views of what constitutes a scientific genre, with particular regard to educational settings. John Dixon (1987) argues that the five textual features specified as scientific by Frances Christie (in a previous discussion of a piece of classroom writing), for instance the use of generalisations, assertions and the 'universal present tense', do not in fact have that function distinctively, and indicate anyway a narrow compliance with one set of notions about science. While agreeing that those textual features 'combine to form a recognisable, indeed well-known, way of structuring prose', he maintains that one could easily 'quote examples of scientific prose ... in which each of the five criteria forming this so-called "genre" were not met, whether severally or collectively' (Dixon 1987, p.12). Science, Dixon reminds us, 'is not an uncontested form of enquiry', and its various possible discursive strategies should offer plenty of choice to students. He develops one hypothetical example of a different pedagogic procedure in order to show 'that alternatives do exist, and that we have to argue first for what we think better (educationally and scientifically) before we decide the (range of) generic choices that may be appropriate—and those that may be disabling' (Dixon 1987, p.13).

In response, Frances Christie (1987) contends (1) that teachers ought to make it quite clear to students that scientific writing does comprise specific linguistic elements, and (2) that we would confuse and therefore disable young students if we were to ask them within the context of a science lesson to write, for example, 'stories' about an observed biological experiment instead of instructing them in the proper generic conventions (Christie 1987, p.26).

I find myself sharing with her the belief that students need to become familiar with the textual features of the most orthodox scientific discourse, but sharing on the other hand with Dixon the belief that students need also to step outside that normative way of framing generically what counts as science. I can summarise my position by saying that scientific (or indeed technological) literacy needs above all to include a *critical* dimension, and that this is best achieved by scrutinising the rhetoric of those textual practices through which science and technology lay claim to truth.[2]

---

2   The following remarks draw extensively on passages that I have written for a study guide in the Deakin University unit HUS803 *Science in Culture*. My thanks to Terry Stokes who developed my interest in 'science as text' and drew my attention to some of the articles mentioned in this section.

This 'rhetoric' is not to be equated simply with elegant stylistic flourishes, fancy tropes and the like. (Indeed, it is by no means confined to written language, though in what follows I concentrate on that mode.) Rather, it is a whole set of persuasive devices, some of which Joseph Gusfield (1978) indicates in his article 'The literary rhetoric of science'. Gusfield's most general point is rudimentary enough: that the verbal medium which scientific discourse must use cannot, of course, be a transparent windowpane through which sheer reality is directly visible. His focus is on the language of scientific papers, and he remarks that, while these seldom draw attention to their artful use of their medium, nevertheless they do not present a purely objective and comprehensive account of the phenomena they examine. Their stance of neutrality—towards subject matter, audience and one's own role as researcher—is an illusory rhetorical effect; that is to say, the very act of making this illusion persuasive involves the author of a scientific paper in a number of devices of selection.

To accept that analysis is to accept certain curricular consequences. If teachers are content to treat scientific writing—or indeed their own classroom discourse—as generically 'given', as comprising a set of what Ruqaiya Hasan calls 'obligatory elements' in the lexico-grammatical structure of a text (Halliday & Hasan 1985, p.61), they encourage students to accept that writing at its own valuation, to take its rhetoric uncritically as legitimating a truth-claim. If, instead, they help students to analyse the textuality of science, not only in its written forms but in oral circulation (including what is said in science lessons), they are fostering what Bill Green (1988) calls 'critical literacy'. By what means do scientific authors, or teachers of science, establish their credentials for knowing about X? From what narratorial or speaking position do they perceive, interpret and present X? What position does the tenor, field and mode of their language ask readers to adopt? Which things are emphasised and which are occluded in the sequencing of reported 'facts'? These are the sorts of questions in which rhetorical analysis specialises. Wayne Booth, who is cited by Gusfield, sums up the general view that literary critics have of a fiction-writer's art when, referring to claims made by Flaubert, Chekhov and others, he says this:

> We all know by now that a careful reading of any statement in defense of the artist's neutrality will reveal commitment; there is always some deeper value in relation to which neutrality is taken to be good. (Booth 1961, p.68)

This general question of the 'deeper value' underlying and motivating an apparently neutral report is discussed by John Law and R.J. Williams (1982). They remark that 'significance or meaning can only be allocated to an element by putting it next to, and seeing it in relation to, other elements' (Law & Williams 1982, p.538); thus, in the particular organisation of a scientific paper, the author's aim:

is to propose a value for the paper, a value for himself, and a value for
the bits and pieces so juxtaposed. It proposes a reality in which events,
facts, and scientists have their place. Power in science, as elsewhere,
comes from the successful capacity to create and impose value. And it
is for this capacity that scientists struggle when they write a paper.
(Law & Williams 1982, p.539)

What does all this imply for education? One important issue is the
kind of informed rhetorical awareness that pedagogic structures and what
Christie (1985) calls 'curriculum genres' can give to students as they
encounter the textuality of science and technology. To be literate in those
domains of knowledge does not merely mean to understand how certain
bits of equipment operate or to be conversant with certain experimental
procedures and findings. Unless the learning is of a self-reflexive kind that
explores such questions as how a technical manual or a scientific paper
claims authoritative status for itself, and why the science and technology
curriculum itself has varied in different times and places, then the
student's literacy will be weak and incomplete. In other words, science and
technology, like literature, need to be understood and taught as textual
practices.

This understanding is linked, of course, with a cluster of issues
concerning the authorisation of knowledge through larger discursive
formations: how professional hierarchies and interest groups influence the
nature of scholarly activity and control the flow of technical information,
how various 'disciplines' and special knowledges are legitimised and
circumscribed, and so on. But an emphasis on textuality leads one to look
closely at the way authority operates at the micro-level of linguistic
choices, in this case *within* different uses of language. Charles Bazerman
(1981) has some interesting observations on this topic in his paper 'What
written knowledge does: Three examples of academic discourse'. Again, the
focus is on the shaping of formal printed discourse; hitherto, there has not
been a great deal of close attention paid to spoken science. But the general
findings here are still instructive. Whereas Gusfield (1978) draws attention
to similarities between scientific writing and imaginative fiction,
Bazerman indicates specific differences between three sorts of 'knowledge-
bearing texts', none of which is 'literary' in the avowedly fictional sense—
though one of them does discuss a poem and does itself go in for 'verbal
play' and 'reverberative density' of style. While Bazerman is careful to
point out that his examples may not be totally representative of papers in
their three fields (natural science, social science and humanities), his
interest is still in the distinctive ways in which knowledge tends to be
constructed by separate disciplinary traditions.

There is no basic conflict between Bazerman's approach and Gusfield's.
Although their purposes and terms are different, both are underlining the
point that science circulates as a textual practice—one that, as Peter
Medawar (1963, p.378) remarks, is not to be identified (despite some of its
rhetorical claims) with 'the way scientists actually think when they come
upon their discoveries' (cf. Charlesworth et al. 1989). Bazerman sees each

114

of his chosen texts as producing a form of knowledge by *framing* itself (my term, not his) in relation to certain contexts. Thus, while we may regard as a mere stylistic detail the chosen perspective of an authorial persona (the way Crick and Watson use the first person plural, or Merton's adoption of a companionly tone, or Hartman's display of cleverness), these are inseparable from the attitude in each case towards accumulated work in the same field—previous literature within its field or 'tradition'.

That last point involves the important textual nexus between authorship and authority, cognate terms that should figure as prominently in the analysis of written scientific research as they do in the analysis of imaginative literary fictions. One seldom meets in literary criticism nowadays the notion that an individual writer's 'originality' is the source of a novel or poem or whatever. Rather, attention is usually directed to the complex weft of artifices and allusions that constitute what is written. Increasingly current as an indicator of this is the term 'intertextuality', used (I quote a standard glossary):

> to signify the multiple ways in which any one literary text echoes, or is inescapably linked to, other texts, whether by open or covert citations and allusions, or by the assimilation of the features of an earlier text by a later text, or simply by participation in a common stock of literary codes and conventions. (Abrams 1981, p.200)

In this perspective, the author no longer has a privileged place. Roland Barthes puts the point provocatively:

> We know now that a text is not a line of words releasing a single 'theological' meaning (the 'message' of the Author-God) but a multidimensional space in which a variety of writings, none of them original, blend and clash. The text is a tissue of quotations drawn from the innumerable centres of culture. (Barthes 1977, p.146)

Another influential contemporary French thinker, Michel Foucault, similarly argues that although a text may include grammatical references to an 'author-function' ('I'), 'neither the first person pronoun, nor the present indicative refer exactly either to the writer or to the moment in which he writes, but rather to an alter ego whose distance from the author varies, often changing in the course of the work'. Moreover, he insists that this is not 'a characteristic peculiar to novelistic or poetic discourse' (Foucault 1979, p.152).

A curriculum, then, that is alert to textuality as something transgressive of generic constraints will want students of science and humanities alike to develop skills in recognising how any writer or speaker tries to combine a claim to personal knowledge with a claim to be operating within a discursive tradition. One simple form that this takes in a scientific paper is the conventional preamble whereby, as Medawar (1963, p.377) describes it, 'you concede, more or less graciously, that others have dimly groped towards the fundamental truths that you are now about to expound'. A comparable point is made by Ross Chambers (1984, p.215) in a recent book on literary fictions when he suggests that a narrator's ostensibly respectful allusion to earlier texts may sometimes carry the implication 'where X was only partially successful, I will do better'. But there are comparable strategies in ordinary oral language as well.

In summary, to textualise the study of science and technology is to devise a curriculum that shows them to be practices mediated through rhetorical language, a curriculum that shows why, as Steve Woolgar (1980, p.248) states, 'it is not possible to retrieve the character of phenomena (specifically, this includes "ideas", "concepts" and "facts") independently of their presentational context'.

Practice and framing

Hitherto, my examples have concentrated on the way texts are seemingly produced by writers and speakers; but of course there is a complementary set of functions whereby readers or listeners interact with those potential texts in order to give them meaning. This process of textual exchange can usefully be considered in terms of the metaphor of 'framing', because every act of meaning-making is shaped by textual practices through the situation in which it occurs, and ought to take account of that fact.

The need to consider the situatedness of interpretation (whether in reading or listening) should be paramount for those whose concern is with what happens in classrooms. It therefore figures importantly in the schematic model of framing that has been developed in work undertaken with school teachers and students by the Centre for Studies in Literary Education at Deakin University. Broadly summarised, this model represents the means by which readers make sense of texts through recourse to several kinds of framing. Some framings are drawn from information seemingly inherent 'within the text' (though notions such as 'within' and 'outside' become problematic here), while some are drawn from the circumstances in which the texts are encountered (e.g. pedagogic and curricular structures) or are fetched from further afield with various degrees of pertinence.

How does this concept of 'framing' differ from concepts of 'coding' expounded by Roland Barthes (1974):[3]

1   In the Barthesian sense 'codes' virtually assume an intricate literary text and a ready-made subtle reader of high literary competence, whereas analysis of 'framing' can indicate how all interpretation works (and incidentally how the particular practices associated with 'literary' reading may be acquired and developed).

---

3   The following paragraphs are based on my chapter 'Reading as framing, writing as reframing', in *Reading and Response* (Reid 1990).

2   The emphasis of Barthes's reading 'codes' is on a relatively formalistic view of textual properties, whereas 'framing' attends more directly to the occasions and processes through which readings and other textual exchanges actually occur.

3   The concept of framing allows, in a flexible way, for the importance of interactive factors (e.g. in classrooms), since these themselves may serve to frame what is read and heard.

4   Codes do not in themselves account for durational and retrospective elements in textual exchanges, but the concept of framing can readily be extended to reframing.

5   'Code' suggests a set of fairly clearcut constituents, whereas the very notion of 'framing' draws attention to the problematic distinction between what is inside textuality, or inside interpretation, or inside a body of knowledge, and what is outside them.

This needs fuller exposition now. To regard our acts of interpretation as acts of framing is to allow full scope to textuality—to recognise that we make a text mean something by both separating it from, and joining it with, a variety of references. The metaphor of framing simply reminds us that in order to perceive and understand anything (whether a techno-logical process, a poem, a science lesson, or an event in the natural world), we must provisionally distinguish it from other things while also relating it to them—as we distinguish figure from ground, picture from wall, poem from page, foreground from background, here from there. Framing is the process of demarcating phenomena in a double-edged way that simultaneously includes and excludes. What makes it provisional is that neither its terms of reference nor its principles of relevance are fixed. As Jacques Derrida (1978, p.83) remarks in an essay on aesthetics: 'Il y a du cadre, mais le cadre n'existe pas'—which I render as this principle: framing occurs, but there is no frame.

Four kinds of framing can be differentiated—though in practice they are not categorically discrete. For convenience, I label these 'circum-textual', 'extratextual', 'intratextual' and 'intertextual'. Please take these terms with a grain of salt and a willing suspension of distaste.

1   *Circumtextual* framing uses the perceived adjuncts of a text in order to make it meaningful. In the case of a printed item, these adjuncts comprise a variety of tangible details that surround it not only with further words, such as a title, but with additional signs and structures to guide interpretation. In so far as we frame a written story circumtextually, we read it in terms of the material borders by which it is palpably constituted: details of its physical format, cover and prefatory information, blurbs, dedications, epigraphs, titles, opening

and closing formulae, authorial ascriptions, marginalia, footnotes, or other such markers. In oral situations, the term 'circumtextual' is equally pertinent; at school, for instance, it may often be applied to certain official and unofficial rubrics that seem to encompass classroom talk: not only what is said about cellular structures in the course of this morning's science lesson, but what was said at the end of the previous lesson about preparing for the big exam; not only what old Bloggs tells you to learn, but what the curriculum handbook requires. The metaphor of circumtextual framing underlines the fact that a firm perimeter cannot always be delineated around a text.

2 *Extratextual* framing includes whatever seemingly 'outside' information, unspecified by the text but felt to be presupposed by it, is brought to its understanding, along with the reader's various expectations and preoccupations. The extratextual framing of anyone's engagement with a particular text is always somewhat arbitrary, depending largely on a personal stock of knowledge and assumptions. Because it encompasses many variable preconceptions as well as different degrees of cultural knowledge, it is responsible for most disagreements between readers. But we should not think of these differences as capriciously individual; they stem from institutionalised textual practices. In any case, however, what makes any particular frame of extratextual reference more or less apt is simply the scope it gives a reader to draw meaning from other framing elements 'in' and 'around' the given text—from circumtextual elements, already mentioned, and from intratextual and intertextual, which I shall now define.

3 For a third kind of framing the term *intratextual* has been coined because it takes shape directly on the pages themselves (or the equivalent, if it is a non-print text), deriving in particular from whatever subdivisional devices interrupt or redirect the flow of words. In a written item, the most obvious of these are spatially emphatic paragraph breaks, section numbers and typographically marked shifts; but anything that can suddenly alter a reader's mode of apprehending the text, such as an abrupt tonal change or some oddity of diction or syntax, may count as material for intratextual framing.[4] One form that

---

4   In a comment following the conference presentation of this paper, David Butt suggested that linguistic analysis can specify important features which my 'framings' fail to cover. His example was a remark by Deirdre Burton on the way Sylvia Plath's writing consistently constructs the role of the woman-in-the-text as 'acted upon'; Burton points to gender implications on the transitivity system in the grammar itself. Yet, in fact, this example perfectly illustrates my point about the way all reading occurs through framing. Burton's remark and Butt's use of it both indicate how a certain set of extratextual knowledges and interests (e.g. in gender, in formal linguistic description) can serve to elicit a certain set of intratextual structures (e.g. a marked syntactical detail) in order to produce an interpretation of that text. There are, of course, many other possible ways of reading a given Plath passage, and it will be framing that makes the difference in each case. If it seems to a particular linguist that the dominance of such and such a meaning is somehow prescribed intrinsically

this takes is the effect of ironic disjunction, differently signalled in speech and writing; another, the staple of metafictional literary artifice, is the tale-within-a-tale, or embedded narrative, which often has the reflexive function of commenting implicitly on the text that encloses it.

4   Finally, *intertextual* framing: this has to do with links between texts but should be understood as involving more than just the casual allusions or traces of 'influence' mentioned in the definition quoted earlier from Abrams. For intertextuality, in the strong sense proposed by Julia Kristeva (see Moi 1986), works through devices by which a text signals how its very structure of meanings depends on both similarity to and difference from certain other types of text, involving a transposition of one sign system (or more than one) into another.

As I said before, these four processes should not be thought of as wholly separate frames. In any approach to any text, the shifting relations between different framing possibilities are always paramount. For instance, an extratextual dimension must be invoked; no text is comprehensible apart from what its readers bring to it; but the important thing is not to be locked preclusively into one or two kinds of extratextual framing. While a particular text may signify its generic affiliations through circumtextual, intratextual and intertextual devices, these will remain invisible unless a reader can draw on appropriate extratextual information. Conversely, it may happen sometimes that assumptions imported into the reading will frame a text too tightly to allow its distinctive contours to be recognised.

In terms of these processes, the research group with which I work has been studying aspects of reading practices in secondary school classrooms. When beginning our investigations, we did not go armed with the elaborate typology that I have just described. What we did have was two strong hunches: (1) that although textual limits and ostensibly unificatory reference points for interpretation may often appear to be 'given' and fixed, this is usually because of limited habits of perception, routinised pedagogic practices, or temporary pragmatic constraints; and (2) that interpretive skills can be enhanced by developing strategies of mobile reframing that address directly the textuality of what is said and heard, read and written. Nor did we see our task as requiring an 'objective' description, by detached observers, of what readers do with texts. Rather, in attempting to understand what happened to texts within a classroom context, we regarded ourselves as part of that context, intervening in students' reading processes rather than watching them from the sidelines. We paid attention to the assumptions they themselves apparently brought to bear on their reading, and explored ways of increasing their awareness

---

by lexico-grammatical features themselves, rather than by a particular reader's use of them to the exclusion of other potential meanings, this demonstrates only how easy it is for one's obsessions to frame interpretation with excessive rigidity.

of alternative possibilities. What we did, then, was partly a kind of curriculum development, involving a critique of some current practices in teaching literature and an exploration of strategies to open up dimensions in reading and writing that traditional courses have tended to suppress.

By those means, framing—in each of the senses discussed earlier—is being brought into the foreground, as is the fact that all circulation of knowledge occurs within certain curricular and technological practices. For reasons already considered, this awareness of framing factors is just as important to foster in science education as in the humanities. But I conclude now with the reminder that teaching itself, and theorising about teaching, are also systemically situated; that they, too, are institutionalised textual practices rather than autonomous individual initiatives. In a recent book entitled *Culture and Government: The Emergence of Literary Education*, Ian Hunter (1988) traces a history of English pedagogy as a state apparatus in which teachers are simply technicians of control.[5] That sombre view seems to challenge the image of educational leadership functions presented in much curriculum theory and summarised in Bill Green's recent article on Garth Boomer's celebration of teachers' power as 'transformative intellectuals' (Green 1988a). What if Boomer is romanticising our role? What if Hunter is right in suggesting that transformations achieved by pedagogy have all been effected in the interest of a '*moral* technology'? Can we devise forms of textual practice that would disturb such a covertly authoritarian curriculum?

References

Abrams, M.H. (1981), *A Glossary of Literary Terms*, 4th edn, Prentice-Hall, Englewood Cliffs, NJ.

Barthes, R. (1974), *S/Z*, trans. R. Miller, Hill & Wang, New York.

Barthes, R. (1977), 'The death of the author', in S. Heath (ed.), *Image–Music–Text*, Collins, Edinburgh.

Bazerman, C. (1981), 'What written knowledge does: Three examples of academic discourse', *Philosophy of the Social Sciences*, vol.11, pp.361–87.

Booth, W.C. (1961), *The Rhetoric of Fiction*, University of Chicago Press, Chicago.

Chambers, R. (1984), *Story and Situation: Narrative Seduction and the Power of Fiction*, University of Minnesota Press, Minneapolis.

Charlesworth, M., Farrall, L. Stokes, T. & Turnbull, D. (1989), *Life among the Scientists*, Oxford University Press, Oxford.

Christie, F. (1987), 'Genres as choice', in I. Reid (ed.), *The Place of Genre in Learning: Current Debates*, Typereader Publications no.1, Centre for Studies in Literary Education, Deakin University, Geelong, Vic.

Christie, F. (1985), 'Curriculum genre and schematic structure of classroom discourse', in R. Hasan (ed.), *Discourse on Discourse:*

5   For reviews of this book, see the journal of the Centre for Studies in Literary Education, Deakin University, Geelong, Vic., *Typereader* no.2 (1989).

Workshop Report from the Macquarie Workshop on Discourse Analysis, Occasional Paper no.7, Applied Linguistics Association of Australia, Sydney.

Derrida, J. (1978), *La Vérité en peinture*, Flammarion, Paris.

Dixon, J. (1987), 'The question of genres', in I. Reid (ed.), *The Place of Genre in Learning: Current Debates*, Typereader Publications no.1, Centre for Studies in Literary Education, Deakin University, Geelong, Vic.

Foucault, M. (1979), 'What is an author?', in J.V. Harari (ed.), *Textual Strategies: Perspectives in Post-structuralist Criticism*, Cornell University Press, Ithaca, NY.

Green, B. (1988a), 'Educational leadership and critical pedagogy: Garth Boomer: A profile', *The Australian Administrator*, vol.9, no.5, pp.1–6.

Green, B. (1988b), 'Subject-specific literacy and school learning: A focus on writing', *Australian Journal of Education*, vol.32, no.2, pp.156–79.

Gusfield, J. (1978), 'The literary rhetoric of science: Comedy and pathos in drinking driver research', *American Sociological Review*, vol.41, no.1, pp.16–34.

Halliday, M.A.K. & Hasan, R. (1985), *Language, Context and Text: Aspects of Language in a Social-semiotic Perspective*, ECS805 Specialised Curriculum: Language and Learning, Deakin University, Geelong, Vic.

Hunter, I. (1989), *Culture and Government: The Emergence of Literary Education*, Macmillan, London.

Lanham, R.A. (1989), 'The electronic word: Literary study and the digital revolution,' *New Literary History*, vol.20, no.2, pp.265–90.

Law, J. & Williams, R.J. (1982), 'Putting facts together: A study of scientific persuasion', *Social Studies of Science*, vol.12, no.4, pp.535–58.

Lyotard, J.-F. (1984), *The Postmodern Condition: A Report on Knowledge*, trans. G. Bennington & B. Massumi, University of Minnesota Press, Minneapolis.

Medawar, P.B. (1963), 'Is the scientific paper a fraud?', *The Listener*, vol.70, 12 September, pp.377–8.

Moi, T. (ed.) (1986), *The Kristeva Reader*, Basil Blackwell, Oxford.

Reid, I. (ed.) (1987), *The Place of Genre in Learning: Current Debates*, Typereader Publications no.1, Centre for Studies in Literary Education, Deakin University, Geelong, Vic.

Reid, I. (1990), 'Reading as framing, writing as reframing', in M. Hayhoe & S. Parker (eds), *Reading and Response*, Open University Press, Milton Keynes, UK.

Ricoeur, P. (1981), 'The model of the text', in J. B. Thompson (ed.), *Paul Ricoeur: Hermeneutics and the Human Sciences*, Cambridge University Press, Cambridge.

Scholes, R. (1987), 'Textuality: Power and pleasure,' *English Education*, vol.19, no.2, pp.69–82.

Thompson, J.B. (1984), *Studies in the Theory of Ideology*, Polity Press, Cambridge.

Woolgar, S. (1980), 'Discovery: Logic and sequence in a scientific text', in K.D. Knorr, R. Krohn & R. Whitley (eds), *The Social Process of Scientific Investigation*, Reidel, Dordrecht, Holland.

Text as curriculum and as technology:
A systemic functional linguistic perspective

Frances Christie

Introduction

I shall start my chapter with a definition and an explanation. Firstly, I want to define what I mean by the term 'text' and its relationship to 'context'. Secondly, I want to explain why for me the scholarly pursuit of the nature of texts is worthwhile. In particular, I shall comment on what I take to be the implications for curriculum theory of the notion of 'text' that is involved. I start in this way because I want to provide a brief overview of the theoretical framework for everything else I shall want to argue.

In a final section of the chapter, I shall make some observations with respect to language and technology. Here, I shall argue that language is itself a technology, and in touching upon this theme, I shall try to link some of what I say to other chapters in this volume.

The notion of 'text'

I use the term 'text', then, as a linguist does, and since linguists themselves often disagree, let me say further that I use the term as a systemic functional linguist does. Here let me quote M.A.K. Halliday on the subject:

> We can define text, in the simplest way perhaps, by saying that it is language that is functional. By functional, we simply mean language that is doing some job in some context ... (Halliday & Hasan 1985, p.10)

The notion of text is meaningless without its associated notion of 'context'. And the notion of context here is itself to be understood in two related senses, both taken from the work of Bronislav Malinowski (1923, 1935). Briefly, Malinowski drew attention to the manner in which the culture in which people operate fundamentally determines the nature of the meanings or the social purposes of the people concerned. Most cultures, for example, have trading encounters of various kinds, though they differ quite markedly from culture to culture. But in addition to that, within any context of culture there will be further marked differences in meanings or social purposes, depending upon the specific context of situation in which we engage at any given time. Thus, within our own culture, for example, the particular instance of the trading encounter that occurs will be dependent upon the specific context of situation in which we operate. Both senses of context need to be borne in mind at all times.

Language has meaning because of the context in which it is used. Conversely, context is comprehensible because of the manner in which it is realised in language. Language, then, is a primary semiotic or symbolic system with which we mean. Hence, for J.R. Firth in 'Linguistic analysis as a study of meaning' (1968) for example, as for systemicists since he first wrote it, the study of language is the study of meaning. Though Firth did not discuss the matter in these terms, I would want to add that the concern with meaning necessarily involves a concern with the ideologies that apply in any given context in which language is used—be they, for example, ideologies to do with the nature of the economy, the nature of knowledge, or the nature of childhood, to name a few which regularly stir people up.

Before I leave the issue of meaning-making in language, I must make one other point to avoid a possible misconstrual which sometimes occurs when it is claimed that language is a meaning system. It is *not* suggested that humans do not use other semiotic systems. We mean—or 'sign', to use another helpful term—in a multitude of ways: in dance, music, painting, sculpture, photography, in our architecture, in our choice of clothes, to mention some obvious examples, all of them of fundamental importance to any notion of a culture however we might want to define the term. But language is a principal semiotic system which the human species has evolved, implicated in quite critical ways in so much of what we think of as daily human endeavour, including, of course, the endeavour of teaching and learning in schools. For that reason alone, the notion of text is absolutely critical to any notion of the school curriculum.

This brings me to the second of the concerns I said I wanted to touch upon in my opening observations, while still defining and indicating something of the theoretical framework with which I work: namely, the reasons for the systemic functional linguist's scholarly pursuit of the nature of text, in particular as that might have implications for curriculum theory. About this, it should be noted that I would need considerably more space to do the subject justice than I have here. I can do no more than sketch in some ideas.

Text and curriculum theory
In a volume about 'genre' edited by Ian Reid, a contribution of mine (Christie 1987) constituted part of an ongoing dialogue in which I had been involved with John Dixon. The latter was uneasy about the notion of

'genre' as I had been developing it, along with a number of others who were working with systemic functional linguistic theory and were associated with the Department of Linguistics at the University of Sydney. They include Jim Martin, Guenter Plum, Joan Rothery and Cate Poynton, to name a few. Space does not permit that I rehearse all the arguments, and readers are advised if interested to read the volume (Reid 1987). I shall pick up just a couple of matters germane to my arguments here. A genre as we define it is a 'staged, purposeful goal-oriented activity'—something undertaken to achieve important goals. As Jim Martin, Joan Rothery and I developed the point in the Reid volume we wrote:

> Genres are referred to as *social processes* because members of a culture interact with each other to achieve them; as *goal oriented* because they have evolved to get things done; and as *staged* because it usually takes more than one step for participants to achieve their goals. (Martin, Christie & Rothery 1987, p.59)

All texts will be marked by some characteristic overall pattern or shape—their generic structure or their schematic structure—itself a cultural artefact, deriving from the context of culture in which people operate. The particular instance of any genre—be it a prestige one such as a sonnet, or a non-prestige one such as a lesson—will be determined by the register of the actual context of situation which applies. That is to say, as I found in a recently completed study of early writing development (Christie 1989b), a characteristic curriculum genre did apply for the purposes of teaching the children to write in the school concerned. There was an identifiable writing planning genre, different from other examples of curriculum genres as I identified these in the school day. However, the particular expression of the writing planning genre in any one instance that I recorded and collected was determined, I argued, by the operation of *register*—of factors which were of the specific context of situation. In fact, though I shall not develop the point here at any length, I should note that I actually argued the presence of two registers, one a pedagogical register, having to do with the ongoing pedagogical purposes of the lessons, the other to do with the particular 'content' selected for teaching the students to write about. A register may be thought of in terms of its *field*—the nature of the social activity involved; its *tenor*—the nature of the relationship of the participants that applies; and its *mode*—the particular role of language in the construction of the text.

Figure 1 attempts to set out the current formulation of the theory, as proposed by Martin (1987) and others.

Ideology, genre and register are each held to be different systems, operating on different planes. In the figure, in the bottom right-hand corner lies language itself, operating as a meaning system. Above it, and in fact standing in parasitic relationship to language, lies register. It is described as parasitic in that it must select from language in order to realise its meanings, since it has no form or expression of its own. Similarly,

125

genre is said to stand in parasitic relationship to register, while ideology stands in parasitic relationship to genre. Ideology, genre and register are said to 'stack up' in relation to language, accounting for the manner in which they are represented in the figure.

Figure 1
Language, register, genre and ideology

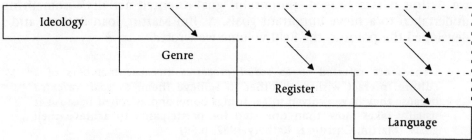

Source: Poynton (1985, p.9).

Elements of register and of genre in any text then, the theory holds, are simultaneously realised in the linguistic choices participants make (though it is not suggested, by the way, that such choices are conscious). And implicit in the operation of genre and register will be significant ideologies of various kinds. To complete this account of the manner in which people like me go about doing our research, I should note that one uses a systemic functional grammar (Halliday 1985a) to analyse the text, and to demonstrate the ways in which the linguistic choices realise both register and genre, and through that analysis, one aims to identify the actual ideologies that operate.

My own study involved a twofold engagement, on the one hand with the curriculum genre in which teacher and young students worked together, and on the other hand with the written genre the students were intended to produce. That is to say, I was concerned with the manner in which teacher and students used language to construct meanings relevant to various tasks for writing, and then wrote. It was impossible, as I early realised, to say anything useful about what was written except by reference to what was said and/or read preparatory to writing. Very early on, then, the issue of intertextuality as Bakhtin (see Todorov 1984) outlined it became of concern to me, though I shall not in fact pursue the point here at any length. I shall say a little more about my study later. First, though, I want to comment on the significance of what I have said for the issue of why *text study* as I and others do it is important, especially for *curriculum theory*.

There are at least two objects of a systemic functional linguistic enquiry into the nature of text of the kind I attempt to do. In the first place, I aim to uncover the manner in which meanings and/or practices are constructed in language. In the second place, I seek to challenge the nature of those meanings and practices, and to work to intervene in order to bring about new ones, where that is a desirable thing. Such an

126

endeavour, I believe, can make an important contribution to the development of curriculum theory and practice. Such an endeavour is itself consistent with a great deal of other contemporary radical theory about the curriculum and curriculum change.

Now that I have made some brief opening observations about the theoretical framework I use and have at least touched upon something of its curriculum implications, I want to move on and take up other matters. I shall begin by taking up one of the matters raised in my discussions with Dixon (1987), and to which Reid makes reference elsewhere in this volume. I take it up because it appears so regularly in discussions about genres and so-called genre-based approaches to the teaching of writing with which people like me in Australia have become associated. I refer to the questions of 'individuality' and 'free choice' in writing and in using language generally.

Free will, choice and genres

One of the early instances of a curriculum genre I collected in which a teacher was preparing her Year 1 children for writing was one in which the teacher displayed a very good children's book called *Egg to Chick* (Selsam 1972). She promoted talk about the book, about its series of illustrations and about at least some of the meanings to do with the development of the chicken in the egg. The lesson occurred as part of an ongoing unit of work which had involved bringing fertilised eggs into the classroom and keeping them in an incubator so that the children might watch the chicks hatch and grow. There were a number of features of the context of situation of the particular lesson which marked the text developed in talk as scientific. For example, to use a technical term from the systemic functional grammar, the *processes* realised in the spoken text were to do with the growth of chicks— how they grow, how they change, how the mother warms them, how they become fully fledged chickens ready and able eventually to break their way out of the egg shell. There were other features, of course, though I shall not repeat these here. Suffice it to note that after a considerable period of talk of how chickens grow, the teacher, all unwittingly, invited the children to write 'stories' about 'how a chicken grows', thereby causing a degree of confusion for several of the young writers involved. One child wrote the following, in which, by the way, I have corrected the spelling:

> Once upon a time a hen lay an egg inside the egg a chicken was being born the chick eats the yolk it makes a little hole now the chick is making a big crack.

This actually starts as a story, and then it drifts into some kind of factual and/or scientific writing, modelled in fact on the discourse generated in the patterns of classroom talk preparatory to the writing. As such, it does not succeed as an effective piece of writing, constituting neither story nor scientific writing.

I argued that the actual meanings appropriate to the context of situation and, indeed to the Western context of culture in which scientists build information about the life cycle of chickens, required the writing of a scientific genre, not a story. I would now call the genre required an *explanation* genre. I also argued that if the teacher herself had had a better developed sense of scientific discourses and of the sorts of genres scientists employed in order to make the meanings of such discourses she would more usefully have pointed the children into writing them. She would, for example, have modelled features of the explanation genre for the children and drawn attention to the manner in which they might put together such a genre.

I have no particular interest in dwelling on this discussion at any length, since I have dealt with it more than once elsewhere, most recently and at length in my doctoral dissertation (Christie 1989a). I want to take up the issues of free choice, individuality and judgments about 'normative' behaviour which I understand Dixon and Reid (elsewhere in this volume) are arguing. Reid writes that he shares with me 'the belief that students need to become familiar with the textual features of the most orthodox scientific discourse', but that, like Dixon, he believes that 'students need also to step outside that normative way of framing generically what counts as science'.

I do not see the issue as one of teaching for 'orthodoxy' or for 'normative' ways of working. On the contrary, the kind of theory I have earlier outlined would argue that, as a matter of participation in many practices involving the construction of texts, we learn to make meanings in various significant ways. The kinds of meanings made, like the manner in which those meanings are realised in texts, are matters determined by the collective social practices: they are not merely orthodoxies, taken up or rejected at will. Hence, to return for the moment to the issue of how chickens develop, I can say that I have studied a number of university texts on the subject, and have interviewed at least one practising biologist who teaches such matters. I can testify that, at least on the basis of such a sampling, the kinds of linguistic choices made by the writer of the children's textbook *Egg to Chick* which was used in the lesson do accord with the choices made in the discourses both of the university texts sampled and of the practising biologist. I would suggest, as I did originally, that the teacher would have done better to have encouraged the children to model their writing on that of the textbook.

Whenever one makes the latter kind of observation, incidentally, one is heard, at least in some quarters, as teaching for 'conformity', or in some way as compromising the rights of individuals to choose. I make two responses to that. In the first place, as I have argued elsewhere, an educational activity is a matter of *initiation*, and in using that term, I mean something very similar to the definition of an education proposed by Fitzclarence (elsewhere in this volume). Initiation involves knowing *how things work and how to use them*, but that in itself does not equal

128

conformity. Secondly, I would suggest that it says much for the ideology of the idealised individual still so well established in Western cultures like our own that the notion of education as initiation is so easily heard as being about conformity, or, in Reid's terms, about 'generic constraint'.

At bottom, the notion that genres impose constraints upon persons arises from a particular ideology of the person or the 'subject'. It is the romantic notion of the person, which has had a long-established place in many discussions about the teaching of English in the nineteenth and twentieth centuries. True, Reid rejects the romantic notions of Wordsworth and others, as well as much twentieth-century 'reader response' theory. However, in that he hears me as proposing genres which represent at best 'orthodoxies' and which at worst appear to impose 'generic constraints', cutting in some way across persons' capacities to move, then I do sense an implicit ideology of the unique or idealised individual or subject in what he says.

Incidentally, I have found it interesting in this connection to read a recent paper of Warwick Mules (1989, pp.26–7), who has suggested the operation of another kind of subject or self in my writing—an 'extra-linguistic self'. Such a self, he says, engages in 'social act(s)' which are 'conditioned by linguistic restraints'. I agree that there is a strong sense of the individual as a social construct in my writing, though I do not in the least accept the interpretation he appears to offer here. Indeed, I find Mules's choice of language quite significant for the implicit sense it carries of the person 'conditioned' and under 'restraint'. I reject this particular reading of what I have argued. Genres are ways of making meaning. They do not impose restraint. On the contrary, they confer capacity to choose to make meanings—*capacity to do things of value and significance*. The notion of the idealised individual operates in Mules's thinking as well.

In a very interesting discussion of the individual, Lemke (1988) has addressed what has become known as 'the problem of the subject'. He seeks to demonstrate that if there is such a problem, it is essentially one of our own making, and of our as yet incomplete attempts to come to terms with the insights of much twentieth-century social theory. He writes:

> Modern critical discourse, in semiotics, literary studies, and social theory, has been struggling for some years now with what we have come to call the 'problem of the subject'. We have fashioned it out of our perplexity over the contradictions between traditional notions of the human individual and newer, essentially social ways of talking about human meaning. Through it we remind ourselves that the modern intellectual revolution remains painfully incomplete. (Lemke 1988, p.1)

As Lemke goes on to argue, much of the problem of 'the subject' is caused by our own enduring liberal bourgeois commitment to such a notion. Once we shift the focus from the traditional and romantic notion of the individual to the individual as a social construct, as Lemke goes on to demonstrate, then many of the arguments about the subject, about free choice and about free will, assume a very different complexion. Since individuals are shaped in social processes, their individuality, I suggest, is actually extended and enriched by the steady acquisition of capacity to undertake different social practices—by capacity if you will, to do more things. Capacity to do more things or to mean in new ways involves capacity to construct new texts.

Learning to construct the genres of one's culture is learning to exercise choices for the realisation of different meanings. This is a *liberating*, not a constraining process.

I have suggested that an educational process is one of initiation, and that this involves knowing how things work and how to use them. For the purposes of teaching genres for writing, this will involve both learning how to recognise the genre by deconstructing it and analysing it, and learning how to construct it in order to mean. To use a metaphor, this is a question of both 'getting inside' the genre and also 'standing outside' it. One needs to do these things in order to understand the genre as well as to challenge it in any of a number of ways, and to use it in order to do new things. Pam Gilbert (1989), for example, is currently interested in studying girls writing narrative genres in which traditional ideologies of gender are turned around.

I see the activities of exploring, deconstructing and constructing genres as an essential part of learning how to use the resources of one's language in order to mean.

All this brings me back to my own study of early writing development, to which I referred earlier.

Learning to use language to make choices

I can here offer only a very compressed discussion of some of the findings of that study. In particular, I must leave the details of the linguistic analysis undertaken to another time. Briefly then, I followed the same population of young children from the preparatory year to the end of Year 2, and I recorded writing lessons every week for three years. I identified a curriculum genre in operation, as I earlier indicated—what I termed a 'writing planning genre'—and I became interested in how children learned the genres for writing that they did. Two matters only I shall comment on. First, teachers always promoted the most discussion about the 'content' of the field or topic for writing. The pattern was remarkable across three years of schooling and some seven different teachers. That is to say, the closer the teacher and children got to talk of the actual writing task, the more underdeveloped was any talk to do with the organisation of the written text the children should write. In fact, the nature of the writing task generally remained implicit to the activity, rather than receiving much explicit treatment. That the teacher always had some kind of unacknowledged notion of the written genre she wanted became clear when she responded to what the children wrote. But the fact was that the actual linguistic choices to be made for writing remained *implicit* to the *teaching/learning situation*. In Basil Bernstein's terms (1975), an 'invisible pedagogy' applied, operating—as all invisible pedagogies do—to the advantage of some and the disadvantage of many others. Where invisible pedagogies apply, there are always some children whose family and social class background prepare them much better than others to understand the processes of text construction and the meanings encoded in such processes that schooling requires and rewards. In the population of children I studied, the children who became the best writers were in fact children of professional families whose first language was English. Those who were less successful were not on the whole from families whose first language was English, nor were they from professional families.

The other matter from my study to which I want to draw attention is that when one examines the written genres actually rewarded in classrooms such as those in which I worked, one finds that two types of genres actually emerged: the *observation* and the *recount*, both of them originally identified some years ago by Jim Martin and Joan Rothery (1980, 1982) in their early work on children's writing. Studies in several parts of Australia (e.g. Christie 1989a; Martin & Rothery 1980, 1981; Walton 1986; Elms 1988; Kamler 1990) testify to the fact that these emerge as the commonest types of genres in a great deal of school teaching practice. They are in fact genres rehearsed in talk, and they are selected by children everywhere in the absence of more overt assistance in learning the many other genres of the written mode. An example of an observation genre, drawn from Barbara Kamler's work, is set out here (spelling and punctuation corrected):

> On the weekend my family got a Christmas tree. We are not going to get the Christmas decorations yet. We have not got it in my house. It is very very little. It has the same pot that we have at home. It is prickly. It has not got a fairy on top of it. Instead it has got a ring on top of it and it has got a bell in the ring. (Kamler 1990)

An example of a recount, drawn from my own study, reads as follows (spelling and punctuation corrected):

> We went to Werribee Part last Wednesday. First we went in the mansion. I liked the pots and the heads on the wall. We saw a stuffed dog. It looked nice and fluffy. Next we went to see the garden. It was a maze. I ran around. Then it was fun. Then we had lunch. Then we saw the ha ha wall. Then we got on the bus. We went back to school. (Christie 1989a)

What characteristically marks such genres is their function in reconstructing aspects of personal experience, normally with some commentary offered upon such experience. The recount differs from the observation principally in that it involves reconstruction of events in terms of their sequence in time (*'first* we went in the mansion'; *'next* we went to see the garden'; *then* it was fun; *'then* we had lunch'; *then* we saw the ha ha wall'; *'then* we got on the bus').

There is nothing wrong in principle with children writing genres whose primary function is to reconstruct personal experience. But close examination of the matter shows that observations and recounts are the genres written by many children more often than any others, very often for several years of schooling. That is because these are the genres practised in a great deal of talk, including such activities as morning talk, and children will inevitably select these if they are offered no opportunity to learn other genres, especially those more relevant to developing control of writing.

So the general point I want to make out of my study is this: that where we leave the written genres of schooling *implicit* to the context of situation, and where we thus do not make them *overt* objects of instruction, we leave significant numbers of students *disempowered*. They are in general disempowered because they are left to deduce the kinds of linguistic choices they must make in order to become competent writers and hence in order, too, to control the kinds of information encoded in such linguistic choices.

I would therefore argue that the linguistic choices students need to exercise in order to control the genres of school learning must become part of the public knowledge of schooling, and not, as they currently are, part of a 'private' and 'invisible' knowledge, selectively available to some students and not to others.

I have suggested here that learning to use language involves learning *to do things*. This is in itself a technological issue, and it is to this that I shall return in my final section.

Language as technology

Language is itself arguably the greatest technology human beings ever invented. We can only speculate on the processes by which language evolved. But evolve it did, out of the other signing systems that humans must have had first, in common with many other animals. For that is what language is—a signing system, a resource or tool for meaning. The emergence of language was a mighty thing in the evolution of the human species, itself making possible the development of many other things we think of as constituting a socioculture, including, of course, the very late twentieth-century technologies such as computers and word processors that have been alluded to by other contributors to this volume.

Though we can never know very much about the emergence of language in the human species, paleontologists, archaeologists and others do tell us that, having invented language as speech, humans walked the earth for many, many centuries before they slowly evolved the first writing systems. In terms of the history of the human species, the invention of writing is itself a recent phenomenon, and for a very long time writing remained the preserve of privileged classes. What is in many ways the more remarkable is the fact that only in very recent times has writing been, potentially at least, available to everyone in societies such as our own, because of the invention of the printing press, and because of the capacity this unleashed for the production of print materials in some quantity. Mass education as it emerged in the nineteenth century would not have been possible without the availability of relatively cheap print materials and the flood of textbooks that appeared over that period.

Kemmis (elsewhere in this volume) refers to the fact that the term 'curriculum' came into use in comparatively recent times—in late eighteenth-century Scotland, in fact. He also goes on to describe the emergence of public and eventually compulsory educational systems in Western countries such as our own during the nineteenth and twentieth centuries, and to suggest that such systems became agencies of state control, parallelling the emergence of modern nation states. Now, among the complex of factors in which I am interested, and which I would argue came to operate in curriculum practices during the nineteenth and twentieth centuries, has been the development of traditions of English language education, the deadening legacies of which remain in many cases today. The effect of such traditions has been to drive language—our most important technology—into the realms of the implicit and the little understood. That is to say, if it is true, as Kemmis suggests, that one effect of the emergence of mass educational systems has been that such systems have emerged as agencies of state control, then one of the most effective means of achieving such control has been the steady loss of traditions of rigorous language study in our schools. That steady loss, I would point out, has produced a generation of teachers of the kind I alluded to in reporting above on my own study—teachers unable to develop sustained discussion of the nature of the genres the students were to write, because the very culture in which they operate has denied them access to such knowledge themselves.

The eighteenth century was a very interesting one from the point of view of the history of attitudes towards language and its teaching, and about this I have written elsewhere (Christie 1981, 1989b, 1990, 1993). The eighteenth century was the last century in which the study of rhetoric held some significance in the history of the British people. Rhetoric was the study of language as a powerful instrument of argument and persuasion, and those of us who work with recently developed approaches to the study of genres are among a number of theorists interested in putting an appropriate interest in rhetorical concerns back into the curriculum.

During the nineteenth century and well into the twentieth century rhetoric died, and an enfeebled tradition of language work, based upon traditional school grammar, came to take its place as the main staple of language studies. Over the same period, and for intimately related reasons, romantic notions not only of the person, but of the writer emerged. Among the complex of reactions to language studies that resulted was the view, for example, that 'great literature' might be admired, but not analysed and understood. The word 'rhetoric' became a term for suspect and shallow practices in using language—a sense in which, more often than not, it is still used today. In other words, anything that suggested an attempt to come to terms in powerful ways with the manner in which language was used for the construction and development of opinion, argument, persuasion and the like became a suspect activity. What is worse, the very people who came in time most strongly to resist efforts to have students engage with language in significant and useful ways were the community of English teachers themselves. I am bound to say, however, that many other teachers do currently hold similar views.

Among the many confusions created by the decline of interest in rhetoric was the loss of much sense of the differences between speech and writing, with what have been unfortunate results. For one thing, written language has often come to be perceived as more important than spoken language. I have more than once been disconcerted by teachers' judgments that transcripts of student talk showed the students were using 'bad grammar'. All this really means is that they are judging speech by the criteria of writing, when in fact the two are different, though the teachers actually lack the knowledge to see the differences. I am not myself convinced, as Reid suggests elsewhere in this volume, that there is a 'traditional opposition' between speech and writing. In fact, I would suggest that once concerns for rhetorically based approaches to language study were lost, then an appreciation of the differences between speech and writing largely disappeared in Western cultures. This is but one aspect of the processes by which the collective knowledge of the technology that is language has been slowly eroded with the growth of mass education in the nation state, to which Kemmis alludes elsewhere in this volume.

Such a loss has led in recent years to, among other matters, the emergence of various 'natural language learning theories' (Cambourne 1986; Cambourne & Turbill 1986), which have proposed that learning to read and write is very similar to learning to talk. Such a proposition is singularly unhelpful for at least two reasons. In the first place, it does not acknowledge the very considerable differences between the spoken and the written modes, about which linguistic studies have had a great deal of use to say (e.g. Tannen 1982; Halliday 1985b). Secondly, even in situations where children are very considerably exposed to print materials, the nature of such exposure never even compares with the nature of their exposure to speech. For this reason alone, writing is learned differently from speech.

Medway (elsewhere in this volume) gives an account of the possible ways in which the impact of the new technologies upon our language system might be explored in classrooms. I would want to endorse the general thrust of his proposals. However, I would add that in my view such explorations will be best undertaken in the context of an overall theoretical framework which focuses on the language system itself as a resource for meaning. Such a framework will allow students properly to address the manner in which different text-types or genres operate for the making of meaning. Where this happens, the general interest Reid (elsewhere in this volume) raises in some exploration of the relationship between speech and writing, as both are being currently affected and changed by the new technologies, could be very usefully addressed.

Finally, I suggest that in the attempt to address the new questions of the curriculum and technology of the late twentieth century, we have to grapple with some problems peculiar both to our species and to our culture. We are the 'talking apes', in Desmond Morris's terms, possessed not only of the primary technology that is spoken language, but of the many other 'secondary' technologies which the primary one has made possible. The effect of our history, especially over the last 200–300 years, has been to develop a Western culture remarkable, on the one hand, for the power which it actually wields over people's lives, and on the other hand, for the manner in which it renders invisible many of its most important instruments of power. Among the latter, we must recognise that language is par excellence an instrument of power.

It is time to break the conspiracy of silence about language that operates so successfully in many areas of our culture, including in our schools. It is time to put the study of language back on the educational agenda. It is time to take seriously the right of our students to know about their language and how it works, so that in learning to use it properly they may exercise the kinds of choices they will need to make if they are to deal intelligently with the truly awesome problems that beset human beings in the modern world.

References

Bernstein, B. (1975), *Class, Codes and Control*, vol.3, *Towards a Theory of Educational Transmissions*, Routledge & Kegan Paul, London.

Cambourne, B. (1986), 'Provide natural learning conditions', in R.D. Walshe, P. Match & D. Jensen (eds), *Writing and Learning in Australia*, Dellasta Books and Oxford University Press, Melbourne.

Cambourne, B. & Turbill, J. (1987), *Coping with Chaos*, Primary English Teaching Association, Sydney.

Christie, F. (1981), The 'received tradition' of English language study in schools: The decline of rhetoric and the corruption of grammar, MA thesis, University of Sydney, Sydney.

Christie, F. (1987), 'Genres as choice', in I. Reid (ed.), *The Place of Genre in Learning: Current Debates*, Typereader Publications no.1, Centre for Studies in Literary Education, Deakin University, Geelong, Vic.

Christie, F. (1989a), Curriculum genres in early childhood education: A case study in writing development, PhD thesis, University of Sydney, Sydney.

Christie, F. (ed.) (1989b), 'Series foreword', Language Education Monographs, Oxford University Press, Oxford.

Christie, F. (ed.) (1990), *Literacy for a Changing World*, Australian Council for Educational Research, Hawthorn, Vic.

Christie, F. (1993), 'The "received tradition" of English teaching: The decline of rhetoric and the corruption of grammar', in B. Green (ed.), *The Insistence of the Letter: Literary Studies and Curriculum Theorising*, Falmer Press, London.

Dixon, J. (1987), 'The question of genres', in I. Reid (ed.), *The Place of Genre in Learning: Current Debates*, Typereader Publications no.1, Centre for Studies in Literary Education, Deakin University, Geelong, Vic.

Elms, M. (1988), A case study in early writing development, MEd Research Paper, Deakin University, Geelong, Vic.

Firth, J.R. (1968), 'Linguistic analysis as a study of meaning', in F.R. Palmer (ed.), *Selected Papers of J.R. Firth*, Longman, London.

Gilbert, P. (1989), 'Stoning the romance: Girls as resistant readers and writers', in Deakin University, *Writing in Schools: Reader*, ECT418 Language Studies: Writing in Schools, Deakin University, Geelong, Vic.

Halliday, M.A.K. (1985a), *An Introduction to Functional Grammar*, Edward Arnold, London.

Halliday, M.A.K. (1985b), *Spoken and Written Language*, ECS805 Specialised Curriculum: Language and Learning, Deakin University, Geelong, Vic.

Halliday, M.A.K & Hasan, R. (1985), *Language, Context, and Text: Aspects of Language in a Social-semiotic Perspective*, ECS805 Specialised Curriculum: Language and Learning, Deakin University, Geelong, Vic.

Kamler, B. (1990), Genre and gender in learning to write: A case study of a girl and boy learning to write, PhD thesis, Deakin University, Geelong, Vic.

Lemke, J. L. (1988), 'Towards a social semiotics of the material subject', in T. Threadgold (ed.), *A Selection of Papers Given at S.A.S.S.C. Seminars, 1986-87*, Sydney Association for Studies in Society and Culture, Working Papers, vol.2, nos 1–2, April.

Malinowski, B. (1923), 'The problem of meaning in primitive languages', in C.K. Ogden & I.A. Richards (eds), *The Meaning of Meaning*, International Library of Philosophy, Psychology and Scientific Method, Kegan Paul, London.

Malinowski, B. (1935), *Coral Gardens and Their Magic*, vol.2, Allen & Unwin, London (reprinted as *The Language of Magic and Gardening*, Indiana University Studies in the History and Theory of Linguistics, Indiana University Press, Bloomington, 1967).

Martin, J.R. (1987), Exporting systemic grammar: Ideology, genre and register in functional linguistics, Mimeo, Department of Linguistics, University of Sydney, Sydney.

Martin, J.R., Christie, F. & Rothery, J. (1987), 'Social processes in education: A reply to Sawyer and Watson (and others)', in I. Reid (ed.), *The Place of Genre in Learning: Current Debates*, Typereader Publications no.1, Centre for Studies in Literary Education, Deakin University, Geelong, Vic.

Martin, J.R. & Rothery, J. (1980, 1981), *Writing Project Reports Numbers 1 and 2*, Department of Linguistics, University of Sydney, Sydney.

Mules, W. (1989), 'Genre theory and hermeneutic questions: A response to the debate', *Typereader*, no.2, pp.25–34.

Poyton, C. (1985), *Language and Gender: Making the Difference*, ECS806 Sociocultural Aspects of Language and Education, Deakin University, Geelong, Vic.

Selsam, M. E. (1972), *Egg to Chick*, A Science I Can Read Book, no. 9, A World's Work Children's Book, UK.

Tannen, D. (ed.) (1982), *Spoken and Written Language: Exploring Orality and Literacy*, Advances in Discourse Processes, vol.IX, Ablex, Norwood, NJ.

Todorov, T. (1984), *Mikhail Bakhtin: The Dialogical Principle*, trans. W. Godzich, Theory and History of Literature, vol.13, University of Minnesota Press, Minneapolis.

Walton, C.E. (1986), Aboriginal children learning to write: Kriol and Warlpiri speakers in an English-speaking classroom, MEd thesis, University of New England, Armidale, NSW.

Poynton, C. (1990) *Language and Gender: Making the Difference*, Sociolinguistic Aspects of Language and Education, Deakin University, Geelong, Vic.

Salem, M.H. (1987) *Eve in Chick, A Science I Can Read Book*, no.?, A Wide-Awake Children's book, UK

Tannen, D. (ed.) (1982) *Spoken and Written Language: Exploring Orality and Literacy, Advances in Discourse Processes*, vol.ix, Ablex, Norwood, NJ

Todorov, T. (1984), *Mikhail Bakhtin: The Dialogical Principle*, trans. W. Godzich, Theory and History of Literature, vol.13, University of Minnesota Press, Minneapolis.

Walton, C.B. (1986) Aboriginal children learning to write: Kriol and Walpiri speakers in an English-speaking classroom, MLitt thesis, University of New England, Armidale, NSW.

Postscript: On curriculum, culture and closure

Rob Walker

In 1959, physicist, science policy adviser, novelist and Cambridge Fellow C.P. Snow gave the Rede Lecture (Snow 1959). He called it 'The Two Cultures', and his argument consisted of a plea for the acceptance of 'science' as a key element in contemporary culture.

Thirty years on, this seems a curious historical oddity. Our lives now seem so deeply dependent on science, science is so much a part of our culture, that it seems strange to suggest otherwise. We have to remind ourselves that when Snow talked of 'culture' to his Cambridge audience[1] he did so, not in the anthropological frame of reference of current usage, but in the sense of 'high culture'. And it was from 'high culture' that he drew the sharpest (some would say, hysterical) criticism from fellow Cambridge academic F.R. Leavis (1962). Leavis took Snow to be talking about culture in the sense of what it means to be 'cultured', rather than in the sense of culture as a set of explicit and implicit social values, and in doing so he rejected science as having anything of intellectual value to offer, particularly when compared with the great works of English literature.

There is no doubt that what in retrospect looks to be a somewhat narrow debate conducted within the confines of the academy had considerable impact. Snow himself noted, in the second edition of his book (Snow 1963), that he was surprised at the public response and suggested that his lecture must have been a trigger for 'an idea whose time had come'.

My own experience tells me this is so. Between 1959 and 1961 I attended two different grammar schools in remote rural corners of Britain, one in North Cumberland and one in West Cornwall (both a long way from Cambridge). In both schools, attempts were made to provide some form of 'common culture' for Sixth Form students, even though the schools had only just sorted us into the arts and sciences. These programs consisted in the main, as I remember them, of lectures (on fine art, on particle physics ...) given to mixed groups of students who had variously

---

1   In fact, his first statement on this theme was three years earlier in the *New Statesman* (6 October 1956).

opted for straight science or straight arts programs. Some of these lectures were very good; at least, they are among a very few things I remember clearly from the curriculum of the time. Nor was the notion of a common culture a passing notion. One school I attended offered a full 'A' level course in 'General Studies' which we were all required to take. And by the time I found myself (in 1961) in a science-based college, enrolled for a straight technology and science degree program, I encountered 'Liberal Studies' as a required program for science students, designed to provide us with access to a broader culture.

For a provincial science student liberal studies was a revelation. The department at Chelsea College included a remarkably able group of teachers, many of whom were destined for greater things. (Those who taught me included Stuart Hall, Harold Silver and Paddy Whanel. Regular visitors included Basil Bernstein, George Melly, George Devine, Maghanita Laski and C.L.R. James). In addition to that advantage, we were within walking distance of the Royal Court Theatre, where some of us became involved in weekly and weekend discussions with writers, actors and musicians, organised by Keith Johnstone, one-time painter and then a playwright and stage director.

Perhaps it is not surprising that routine lectures in organic and physical chemistry began to lose their appeal. And it is true what Snow had said: it did look like two cultures which did not communicate with each other. The problem that loomed for a number of us was how we might sustain some small role in the culture of the arts, while earning a living in the world of science.

I began to understand, too, why Leavis took such great exception to the suggestion that science might be included in what it meant to be cultured. David Suzuki (1990) has recently reminded us that most scientists are employed in the war/defence industries or by multinational companies. In view of the fact that most science is intended to improve our ability to kill or to profit (and frequently both), it is hardly surprising that those whose concerns were with 'culture' defined by 'sensibility' preferred to keep their distance.

There is no doubt that the divide between the arts and science still exists, though not in quite such a strong form. With the benefit of hindsight, the 'two cultures' debate seems somewhat precious. It was clearly located in the British class structure at a crucial point in its history. Snow mentions briefly that science provided a point of access to 'culture' for working-class boys, and in the later edition points to the loss of talent stemming from the fact that the system all but prevented women from gaining access to scientific careers. But these points were drowned out in the noisy debate that followed.

Looking back, I am struck by the multiple dualities that were telescoped into the notion of 'two cultures'. On the surface is the Snow–Leavis debate over the relative merits of science and literature as 'culture', but just below the surface are social class, notions of progress versus tradition, reason versus feeling, objectivity versus subjectivity, the language of the first person versus that of the third person, and so on. It is no accident that the debate occurred at a time when the impact of science was becoming a major social influence. Moreover, it was a time when grammar-school educated working-class students were arriving in the universities in some numbers, when the expansion of the universities was beginning, when television was starting to open 'culture' to mass audiences, and when a new generation was beginning to reconstruct the arts in the wake of the Second World War.

Why return to the debate now? I have to admit that my interest is partly biographical. The debate has left its mark. There is also a fear that some of what was gained in this period is in danger of being lost, especially in Britain. More importantly, it would seem that enough time has passed to return to some interesting issues that have been overlooked and perhaps to rescue some ideas from the wreckage.

The distinction between the arts and the sciences now looks to be a hindrance rather than a help. For education, a major concern must be to find ways of getting past a barrier that confines both cultures to roles that are restricting and, in the case of science, ultimately dehumanising. But how can we begin to do so? The challenge is not resolved by the liberal studies solution of providing points of access to both cultures, since this simply passes the problem to the individual. What is needed is *cultural reconstruction*, more generally, so that the distinction no longer exists in so significant a form.

Peter Medway (elsewhere in this volume) mentions one possible way of doing this when he draws parallels between the 'design process', as it is conceived by engineers, and 'writing', as it is conceived by contemporary advocates of 'process writing'. Another point I would like to raise concerns the outer limits of writing, namely visual imagery, for it is characteristic of much science that its communicative currency is not 'literary' or verbal, but visual, spatial and mathematical. So, too, of course, are painting, sculpture and music, so perhaps there are also points of synthesis and connection beyond language. There are occasional signs that 'normal' science may have reached the limits of its current paradigm. The interest that a few theoretical physicists have shown in Eastern thought may be seen as simply the activities of a lunatic fringe, but, sooner or later, the great expansion of science we have seen in the past fifty years is going to run out of steam and will have to search elsewhere for new ideas. One place to begin is in the limitations of language itself, for it is language that defines the limits of imagination, as Wittgenstein observed.

The design process

The 'design process' has become a key feature of a number of technology education projects in Britain. It lay at the heart of the Schools Council's 'Project Technology' in the early 1970s, and it has been important in the work of the Technology Faculty at the Open University.[2] Once when I asked a teacher to define it for me he said it was best defined by examples,

---

2 See Walker (1980) and MacDonald and Walker (1976).

and the one he gave me was of the science teacher who was installing central heating in his house. He ordered a quantity of small-bore copper piping to be delivered to his house, but forgot that he was going away on holiday. Just as he was leaving home (having given the key to a neighbour who had then left for work), a truck arrived and unloaded the tubing. He could not think what to do with it, but solved the problem by feeding the tubing through the letter flap in the front door.

Of course, there is a lot of technology that does not reduce to design and problem solving. This was nicely illustrated by the head teacher of a boys secondary modern school to whom Barry MacDonald once spoke when we were following the impact of 'Project Technology'. The story he told was of a project on which three schools had collaborated. The aim of the project was to build a boat that would clear weeds from a nearby stretch of canal. The public school had organised the project, the grammar school had made the cutting gear that was mounted on the boat, and the secondary modern school had built the boat. 'How did it work out?', we asked. 'The boat sank', he replied, 'just like "Project Technology".' It would not be hard to imagine similar things happening in the Victorian system.

Elsewhere in this volume, Peter Medway talked about problem solving and design in the context of writing as a 'technology of ideas'. This is an intriguing idea, both practically and because it disrupts the Snow–Leavis debate, suggesting that writing and engineering may share common concerns and common problems. But when we think about finding links between the technologies of materials and the technologies of ideas, it is important that we do not forget the deep structure of social class. Who has the opportunity to write what, in what form, with what purpose to whom? Who creates and who consumes? What social relations are created by the means of production and communication of various texts? These questions would seem to be of greater contemporary interest than the somewhat precious arguments of the 1960s.

These 'new' questions raise some critical issues for those of us in education as we face a range of pressures to relate more closely to the worlds of commerce, employment and money. Do we simulate and replicate existing patterns of social relations, or do we try to change them? Perhaps surprisingly, Snow had a nice answer. In the closing pages of the second edition of his book, he writes:

> Changes in education will not, by themselves, solve our problems: but without those changes we shan't even realise what the problems are. (Snow 1963, pp.99–100)

One final point: the second edition of Snow's book was published in 1963, a date which has considerable personal resonance, for, in 1963, following the Cuban missile crisis, I abandoned my training as a technologist and began afresh in the social sciences. Perversely perhaps, this led me to Karl Popper's lectures in scientific method, which began to provide some basis for making sense of a number of the fragments I have mentioned here.

References
Leavis, F.R. (1962), *Two Cultures?: The Significance of C.P. Snow*, Chatto & Windus, London (first published in the *Spectator*, 9 March).

MacDonald, B. & Walker, R. (1976), *Changing the Curriculum*, Open Books, London.

Snow, C.P. (1959), *The Two Cultures and the Scientific Revolution*, Cambridge University Press, Cambridge.

Snow, C.P. (1963), *The Two Cultures: And a Second Look*, Cambridge University Press, Cambridge.

Suzuki, D. (1990), *Inventing the Future*, Allen & Unwin, Sydney.

Walker, R. (1980), 'Project Technology', in L. Stenhouse (ed.), *Curriculum Research and Development in Action*, Heinemann, London.

A concluding note: Prospects for further enquiry

Bill Green

What is to be done? What are some of the research possibilities in the area of curriculum, literacy and technology, as a single integrated field of enquiry? The principal aim of this monograph has been to open up aspects of the debate and to suggest some ways in which the relationship between language and technology, each broadly and flexibly conceived, connects with and has an impact on education. In this concluding statement, I want to build on and extend the foundations already laid in the monograph and suggest some further prospects for enquiry.

With regard to *curriculum*, for instance, one might usefully explore the significance of the relationship between technology and textual practice, by studying the impact of technological change on curriculum and literacy alike. The most obvious task would be to undertake a comparative study of the printing press and the computer, as arguably the two most important technological forms shaping educational practice. Moreover, as is becoming increasingly clear, the introduction of computer-based technology into education heralds the same kind of curriculum transformation with which the printing press was originally associated, and conceivably could have the same kind of effect on social relations, cultural politics and cognitive processes.

Such a comparative study might be approached by linking the emergence and consolidation of what David Hamilton (1989) describes as the modern classroom system, within the general project of modern(ist) schooling, to the institutionalisation of 'essayistic' forms of literacy—that is, a distinctive relation between textuality and rationality, such that a particular ideology of 'reason' was enshrined in school literacy, culminating in what some would see as the privileging of expository genres at the expense of other forms of textuality and rationality, and other orders of knowledge. That a strong case can be made that significant forms of exposition and argument are of the utmost educational significance, and hence warrant an even greater and more rigorous emphasis in schooling and literacy pedagogy than is currently the case, does not engage the following points.

Firstly, in what can be called its positive thesis, such an argument rests upon the valorisation of a particular view of rationality, one which is deeply embedded in Western ideologies of science and technology, and which has been described as highly masculinist in character. Secondly, the evidence is that, despite their cognitive power, literacy practices of the essayistic kind are more often than not realised in actual school practice in extremely limited forms, as in the ubiquitous 'school essay', institutionalised in the United States in formulaic terms as a 'five-paragraph' structure but clearly discernible in British and Australian schools as well. My point is that it would be particularly generative to undertake such a study as outlined above, both for what it would reveal in curriculum-historical terms and for the illumination it would cast upon such contemporary issues as the significance of linguistic theories of register and genre for literacy and learning, such as debated elsewhere in this monograph. This would be much enhanced by relating these kinds of enquiry, informed as they are by the educational significance of the printing press and its associated technologies, to those likely to emerge in the very near future, given the increasing significance of computer-based technologies in and for schooling.

With regard to *technology* as a conceptual focus, one might well explore the growing importance of technology studies in schools, and indeed the emergence of technology as a school subject in its own right. That is to say, current moves of this kind, in Australia and in the United Kingdom for instance, offer a golden opportunity to study the way in which school subjects are formed, and the curriculum and cultural politics associated with this formation. Such a study would be a contribution to sociological and historical studies of curriculum and schooling, specifically those forms of curriculum research associated with the theory and social history of school subjects and the politics of school knowledge more generally (Goodson 1988; Popkewitz 1987).

Conversely, one might examine the curriculum realisations and manifestations of technology. How might technology best be studied in school settings? Given the view that curriculum involves selection from the available cultural field, what selections are characteristically being made from the culture of technology, and for what reasons? To what extent does the study of technology lend itself to an emphasis on propositional knowledge? To what extent is it conducive to experiential knowledge? Should technology studies combine a practical and vocational emphasis with one which engages questions of culture, history and politics? To what extent does combining a practical and a vocational emphasis entail developing pedagogies which stress both cultural criticism and cultural apprenticeship, whereby students enter into the culture of the technology in question and become practitioners, and at the same time develop a critical-contextual sense of what it is they are working with and studying? This matter might be approached by arguing, as Garth Boomer (1987) does, that a comprehensive technology curriculum needs to provide a balanced program in each of these three emphases: *learning technology* (that is, learning how to use technology, from the microwave oven to the personal computer),

146

learning through technology, and *learning about technology*. Moreover, it would seek to present these in relation to each other.

A similar argument can be applied, of course, in each of these respects to the emergence of computing as a significant feature of contemporary schooling, and one likely to become even more significant in the future. Just as technology is emerging as a school subject in its own right, so too is computing, whether described as 'computer studies', 'computer science' or 'computer literacy'. Against this subject-specific emphasis is a concern for computing-across-the-curriculum, which parallels the argument for the embedding of technology in the school curriculum generally, at every level and in every subject. We might ask if the curriculum of the future should have a separate emphasis on each of these matters—that is, technology and computing—which would require considerable curriculum space. Should there be a distinction made between the two? If so, which should have priority over the other, and why?

These and related questions are generated as a result of the possibility, to say the least, that technology and computing will become 'core' subjects, obligatory elements in compulsory schooling, at the expense of some of those currently regarded, and indeed in some cases legislated, in this way. What subjects in the current array would be displaced or marginalised, and conceivably disappear altogether in the worst-case scenario? There is already some indication, for instance, that this might well be the fate of 'English', certainly in its traditional formulation. Questions that would need to be asked then would be: How much emphasis in the new technology curriculum is placed on the increasing significance of information and communications technology? To what extent would matters relating to language, information and communication, in the context of the technological complex, be taken into account? And to what extent would there need to be an emphasis on the acquisition of specific skills in this regard? This would involve a new combination of 'literacy' and other related skills, in short, although possibly transformed at the point where new competencies and capacities relating to and formed out of media culture, begin to emerge.

Such questions are likely to become ever more insistent as time passes, and as what can be called, after James Carey and John Quirk (1989), 'the rhetoric of the technological sublime' materially registers in education policy and public debate. Already, this is much advanced in Victoria and New South Wales, as in the United Kingdom, in the context of national curriculum development and the triumph of vocationalism and the performativity principle.

Finally, with regard to *textual practice* as a focus, specifically in the context of curriculum and technology and the relationship between them, we might enquire into the changing nature of textuality itself, as well as the significance of textuality in and for schooling. This enquiry would involve study of the cultural and epistemological consequences of those textual practices associated with speech and writing respectively, with the latter commonly seen as the primary and particular concern of the school. This is because literacy, understood for the moment simply as a specific set of competencies and capacities associated with the features and resources of written language, is at once the general *goal* of schooling and its principal *means*. That is, a major outcome of schooling, and arguably the fundamental task with which it is charged, is the achievement of an adequate standard of literacy, in accordance with a relatively arbitrary scale of measurement. So, to date, successful schooling might be understood in terms of a 'media-shift', from speech to writing. Such a shift raises questions about the status and function of the spoken word in the classroom and the school, as well as about the relationship between school culture and popular culture, which involve quite different knowledge bases described by Stephen Ball (1987) as 'elite' and 'mass', respectively, in their orientation.

Furthermore, the new electronic language practices, for instance those associated with television, will have an increasing impact on the established forms of curriculum and literacy, thereby changing them, as well as the social forms associated with them. As a result, mainstream schooling itself will need to adjust, and to position itself in a more interactive and symbiotic relation to media culture, broadly defined. Already, in fact, we can see an increasing emphasis on media as educational practice, both formally and informally.

A further matter to consider is the relative emphasis on 'reading' and 'writing' in literacy education and school practice. Traditionally, the emphasis has been very much on the former, on reading at the expense of writing, and hence on 'consumption' rather than 'production'. As various commentators have noted, it is clear that there are political implications in the preference of one over the other, suggesting that the relationship between school literacy and social discipline and even social control needs to be taken into account. Further, as Cary Bazalgette (1988) notes, mass schooling is notable for its emphasis on 'print literacy', at the expense of a much broader concern with 'media literacy'. She points out that there is a curious anomaly in schooling, in that while print literacy has clearly been the privileged form, it has related even more specifically to 'reading', since 'the possibility that working-class children might learn to produce print as well as consume it was never considered'. Bazalgette extends this point in the following way:

> ... the corollary of learning to read print was learning to write by hand. The notion that print and handwriting were both media, which differ in terms of their status, their necessary technologies, the audiences they can reach, and who has access to them, was not considered important, and on the whole still isn't. The 'competent consumer' became the taken-for-granted baseline for print literacy. (Bazalgette 1988, p.12)

Such arguments clearly warrant further investigation. For the moment, it is sufficient simply to note them here. Clearly, there is much to be done, specifically with regard to engaging and understanding the emergent field of enquiry and action that is language, technology and education. In what follows, then, I want briefly to outline several matters, as theses to be explored.

The first is that literacy might be usefully reconceptualised specifically in terms of the nexus of curriculum, technology and textual practice. That is to say, literacy as both a learned capacity and a social ascription, both a social *institution* and a social *practice*, emerges out of the forging of specific relationships between, on the one hand, teaching and learning, and on the other, reading and writing, with reference to and as shaped by available technologies. More abstractly, we might consider curriculum as a specific system of ideological communication, involving social reproduction and transformation, on one level, and the shaping of student learning on another. 'Reading' and 'writing' might be seen as activities pertaining to written language and written textuality, *and* as metaphors specific to human activity in what is appropriately described as *the written world*, in accordance with the technologies that are available at particular historical moments, of both 'cultural' and 'material' kinds, which enable both curriculum and textual practice to be realised in the ways they are.

One might therefore explore the technologies of print, including the printing press itself (Eisenstein 1985) in relation to particular forms of curriculum and schooling, including 'simultaneous instruction' and the modern classroom system (Hamilton 1989; Goodson 1988), as well as text-based forms of social and educational management, the techniques and ideologies of 'essayistic literacy' (Olson 1988a, 1988b), the construction of the bourgeois individual via text-based 'practices of the self', and the relationship between literacy and assessment, via concepts such as the 'examination' (Foucault 1977). The same kind of analysis, taking into account the specifics in each instance of curriculum, technology and textual practice, can be developed in relation to computing, with reference to the combined effects and implications of word processing, database, email, telecommunications (including 'tele-conferencing' and 'telematics', and 'tele-pedagogy' more generally), hypertext and hypermedia, desktop publishing, and graphics software, among much else.

It is also possible to consider something like 'workplace literacy' in these terms, not just that which is conducted in formal educational settings (TAFE etc.) but also in the workplace itself, increasingly abstracted and textualised as that is (McCormack 1991). The same attention can be given, analytically, to the way in which work-based teaching and learning ('on the job') is both organised by and increasingly focused on particular information technologies, involving various combinations of text, sound and image, and realised in and through specific reading and writing activities, both literally as well as those which are less overtly connected with written language but nonetheless associated with it, in the increasing emphasis on forms of mediation and abstraction.

The second thesis I want to propose is that it would be generative to explore in a more explicit and focused way the specifically *technological* dimensions of both curriculum and literacy. Indeed, understanding curriculum and literacy as themselves 'technologies' is likely to prove illuminating, providing that a flexible and informed view of technology shapes such enquiry. For instance, I suggest that Ursula Franklin's (1990) practice-oriented understanding of technology in terms of what she presents as the two quite different organising metaphors of 'production' and 'growth' is particularly useful in this regard. The first she associates with what she calls 'prescriptive technologies' and links it to notions of standardisation, efficiency and control; the second she links with what she calls 'holistic technologies', which are seen as localised and 'process'-oriented, in the sense that the locus of control with regard to the 'product' remains with those involved in the technological practice in question. The key issue is one of *scale*, related to which are the problems of organisation and institutionalisation. The connections between Franklin's account of 'prescriptive technologies' and Foucault's concepts of power and discipline are very clear, and so are the educational implications and applications (Bigum & Green 1993). Curriculum and literacy in their traditional, modernist forms are very much instances of 'prescriptive technology', as is schooling itself. While Franklin does not develop the educational implications of her argument beyond a certain point, there seems little doubt that the 'mindset' associated with state-sponsored mass compulsory schooling is readily amenable to analysis along these lines. So, too, arguably, are current initiatives to foreground 'competencies' and 'training' in education generally, notwithstanding 'post-Fordist' rhetoric about 'flexible learning' and the like.

Another point to consider here is that, by and large, the significance of technology in and for both curriculum and literacy, as well as the relationship between them, has been missed, or at least greatly undervalued. As suggested previously, neither curriculum nor literacy can be properly understood without due reference to their technological infrastructure, properly conceived. This infrastructure ranges from actual material forms of technology to those which are less immediately or materially apparent as such but present and pervasive all the same. The relatively recent foregrounding in education of technologies such as those associated with computing obscures the fact that there have always been technologies operating in schools and classrooms, while at the same time it focuses attention on what is arguably only one level of technological realisation: the artefact itself, in this case the actual set of materials making up both 'hardware' and 'software'. Yet, as many commentators have observed recently, this is a limited and limiting view of technology, and one which needs to be supplemented by a richer sense of context and practice.

Judy Wajcman (1991), for instance, describes technology as the combination of a form of knowledge, a set of associated human activities and practices, and particular artefacts or 'physical objects'. In the first instance, as she writes, 'technological "things" are meaningless without the "know-how" to use them, repair them, design them and make them. That know-how often cannot be captured in words. It is visual, even tactile, rather than simply verbal or mathematical. But it can also be systematized and taught, as in the various disciplines of engineering' (Wajcman 1991, p.14). In the second instance, ' "Technology" also refers to what people do as well as what they know' and so 'an object such as a car or a vacuum cleaner is a technology rather than an arbitrary lump of matter because it forms part of a set of human activities', just as 'a computer without programs and programmers is simply a useless collection of bits of metal, plastic and silicon'. Finally, 'at the most basic level there is the "hardware" definition of technology', which refers to 'sets of physical objects, for example, cars, lathes, vacuum cleaners and computers' (Wajcman 1991, pp.14–15). The point to be emphasised, though, is that it is this third aspect, literally 'the most basic level', which traditionally has drawn most attention, being in a sense the most concrete level of realisation and definition. Yet it is only when the more abstract considerations of *context* and *practice* are taken into account that the fullest and most appropriate understanding of technology is possible.

This, however, is only one aspect, albeit extremely important, of what I want to describe as the problem of 'invisible technology', in relation to curriculum and literacy. The other is that technologies themselves, even as objects and artefacts, tend to become 'invisible' and to fade into the background, to the point where they are so taken for granted and naturalised that they seem not to exist or to be operating at all. To an extent, this is entirely functional and indeed desirable. As Ihde (1982, p.58) asserts, 'for a technology to function well, it must itself become a barely noticed background effect. It must itself "withdraw" so that the human action that is embodied through the technology can stand out'. For example, it is arguably only in the early stages of learning to write that one is focally aware of the writing instrument as a 'thing' in itself. As one learns to write, the attention increasingly shifts from the instrument (the pencil or pen, or the computer) to the writing itself, and not so much to the physical activity as to the combination of text and task in the production of written meaning. It is only at moments of 'breakdown' that this material aspect of writing becomes apparent again, at least in the usual circumstances of writing—the pen runs dry, or the pencil becomes blunted or breaks off at the point, or—in the case of computing—a fuse blows.

I want to suggest that while this example makes the whole issue of 'invisible technology' or 'technological transparency' seem unexceptional and even entirely innocuous, we might well reconsider the value of making the role of technologies in human practice *more visible*, at least some of the time, so as to highlight the fact that technologies are not neutral and that, rather, they have transformative effects in and on human practice, including writing. Not only is this likely to encourage a meta-awareness of the activity itself, in a similar way with technology as with language, but it also helps keep the social and cultural dimensions of the activity in view, in its entirety. Thus, in turn, where appropriate, people become attuned, as a matter of habit, to the way in which all human activity is framed historically and politically, since technology is 'non-neutral' not just in the practical philosophical sense but also because inevitably a commercial and industrial infrastructure is involved.

The impact of the computing industry on education is particularly illustrative of this process, as Chris Bigum (1992) has argued recently.

Another example is provided by Sean Cubitt (1991), in his account of video culture:

> There is no reason why domestic formats should not deliver far higher quality than the standard Betamax or VHS playback. These have been developed as the lowest common denominator and delivered in sufficient bulk, and therefore at low cost, to saturate the market and remove the possibility of other standards 'competing' for an improved commodity. (Cubitt 1991, p.8)

As he continues:

> Capitalism does not, cannot understand the delivery of quality as a central motivation: the profit motive alone provides its drive. In consequence, most domestic playback is poor, and the sound in particular execrable. We have paid for domestic convenience with a major drop in standards from the clarity and scale of sound and image in the heyday of the cinema. (Cubitt 1991, p.8)

Hence, the shift from cinema to video with regard to cultural practice has been 'transformative' not only in and of itself but also because it was over-determined by commercial interests and the logic of the commodity. The question is, then: how does this effect manifest itself also in education, with regard to its 'technologies'?

A further and final consideration is that 'visibility' and 'invisibility' are often relative matters. As Basil Bernstein's (1977, pp.116–56) analysis of what he calls 'visible' and 'invisible pedagogies' shows very clearly, in specific relation to education, class and social control, the way in which 'visibility' is itself determined and deployed has an unmistakably political dimension, and is closely related to the nexus between authority and hierarchy. This observation suggests that attending to the problem of 'invisible technology' as a matter for critical analysis may have a similar significance. It is worth noting, in fact, that language, pedagogy and technology have always been subject to marginalisation, as well as to the assignment of secondary or supplementary significance, in much social and cultural analysis to date, including that associated with and focused on education. It should be noted that each of these is the 'other' of a binary pair, with the first term in each pair being characteristically and traditionally privileged in both theoretical discussion and general debate: thought/language, research/pedagogy, science/technology. Binary thinking is recognised as a deep-seated feature not only of modernist rationality but of Western logocentric culture more generally, as Jacques Derrida (1976) has argued. It should also be recognised as the logic upon which information-processing models of computing and artificial intelligence is based, a point which needs to be taken into account in assessing the cultural implications of current moves towards the technologisation of education and society.

In conclusion, a point that I hope has become more and more apparent and even insistent in the course of this discussion, and in the monograph more generally, is the parallels and indeed the intrications between language and technology. Hence, there are important associations and connections to be made, I suggest, between language studies and technology studies, on the one hand, and between language education and technology education, on the other. Furthermore, the case for such dialogue becomes even stronger, it seems to me, when consideration is given specifically to the new technologies and concepts such as 'the mode of information' (Poster 1990), where the relationship between language and technology becomes particularly significant. Here, it is pertinent to refer more specifically to *postmodernism* as a frame of reference for educational theory and practice, since it is arguable that what is at issue is a new emphasis on problems of language, information and representation, in social life and social theory alike.

Given this, consider the following statement, from Donna Haraway:

> The extraordinary close tie of language and technology could hardly be overstressed in postmodernism. The 'construct' is at the centre of attention; making, reading, writing, and meaning seem to be very close to the same thing. (Haraway 1991, pp.207–8)

This seems an eminently appropriate note to end on, then, connecting as it does with many of the themes and issues raised in this monograph as a whole. It is indeed timely to take account of the intersections and overlappings of language, technology and education, as a matter of demonstrably central concern in the critical and informed assessment of current policy moves and initiatives, with due regard to what I believe can appropriately be called postmodern educational culture, in all its complexity and ambivalence. What this means in practice, for educators generally, remains to be worked through.

References

Ball, S. (1987), 'Relations, structures and conditions of curriculum change: A political history of English teaching 1970–1985 (1)', in I. Goodson (ed.), *International Perspectives in Curriculum History*, Croom Helm, London.

Bazalgette, C. (1988), ' "They changed the picture in the middle of the fight": New kinds of literacy', in M. Meek & C. Mills (eds), *Language and Literacy in the Primary School*, Falmer Press, London.

Bernstein, B. (1977), *Class, Codes and Control*, vol. 3 *Towards a Theory of Educational Transmission*, 2nd edn, Routledge & Kegan Paul, London.

Bigum, C. (1992), 'Enduring fictions and fantasies: Marketing a future for the new myth information technologies in schools', Faculty of Education, Deakin University, Geelong, Vic, mimeo.

Bigum, C. & Green, B. (1993), 'Technologizing literacy; or, interrupting the dream of reason', in A. Luke & P.H. Gilbert (eds), *Literacy in Contexts: Australian Perspectives and Issues*, Allen & Unwin, Sydney.

Boomer, G. (1987), *Changing Education: Reflections on National Issues in Education in Australia*, Commonwealth Schools Commission, Canberra.

Carey, J.W. with Quirk, J.J. (1989), 'The mythos of the electronic revolution', in J.W. Carey, *Communication as Culture: Essays on Media and Society*, Unwin Hyman, Boston, Mass.

Cubitt, S. (1991), *Timeshift: On Video Culture*, Routledge/Comedia, London.

Derrida, J. (1976), *Of Grammatology*, trans. G. C. Spivak, Johns Hopkins University Press, Baltimore, Md.

Eisenstein, E.L. (1985), 'On the printing press as an agent of change', in D.R. Olson, N. Torrance & A. Hildyard (eds), *Literacy, Language, and Learning: The Nature and Consequences of Reading and Writing*, Cambridge University Press, Cambridge.

Foucault, M. (1977), *Discipline and Punish: The Birth of the Prison*, trans. A. Sheridan, Penguin, Harmondsworth, UK.

Franklin, U. (1990), *The Real World of Technology*, CBC Enterprises, Toronto.

Goodson, I. (1988), *The Making of Curriculum: Collected Essays*, Falmer Press, London.

Hamilton, D. (1989), *Towards a Theory of Schooling*, Falmer Press, London.

Haraway, D.J. (1991), *Simians, Cyborgs, and Women: The Reinvention of Nature*, Routledge, New York.

Ihde, D. (1982), 'The technological embodiment of media', in M.J. Hyde (ed.), *Communication, Philosophy and the Technological Age*, University of Alabama Press, Tuscaloosa.

McCormack , R. (1991), 'Framing the field: Adult literacies and the future', in F. Christie, B. Devlin, P. Freebody, A. Luke, J.R. Martin, T. Threadgold & C. Walton, *Teaching English Literacy: The Preservice Preparation of Teachers to Teach English Literacy*, vol.2: *Papers*, Centre for Studies of Language in Education, Northern Territory University, Darwin.

Olson, D. (1988a), 'From utterance to text: The bias of language in speech and writing', in E.R. Kintgen, B.M. Kroll & M. Rose (eds), *Perspectives on Literacy*, Southern Illinois University Press, Carbondale (orig. pub. 1977).

Olson, D. (1988b), 'Mind, media, and memory: The archival and epistemic functions of written text', in D. de Kerckhove & C.J. Lumsden (eds), *The Alphabet and the Brain: The Lateralization of Writing*, Springer-Verlag, Berlin.

Popkewitz, T.S.. (ed.) (1987), *The Formation of the School Subjects: The Struggle for Creating an American Institution*, Falmer Press, London.

Poster, M. (1990), *The Mode of Information: Poststructuralism and Social Context*, Polity Press, London.

Wajcman, J. (1991), *Feminism Confronts Technology*, Allen & Unwin, Sydney.